THE SECURITY OF CHINA

Chinese Approaches to Problems of
War and Strategy

THE SECURITY OF CHINA

Chinese Approaches to Problems of War and Strategy

Arthur Huck

COLUMBIA UNIVERSITY PRESS

New York 1970

for

THE INSTITUTE FOR STRATEGIC STUDIES

London

Published 1970 in Great Britain by Chatto & Windus, Ltd., London, and in Canada by Clarke, Irwin & Co., Ltd., Toronto

Arthur Huck is an Australian. He visited China in 1965 and 1966. At present he teaches Chinese Politics at the University of Melbourne.

355.03355 1
H 8825

163393

PREFACE

This essay was written after a period of study and discussion at the Institute for Strategic Studies in London. The participants in these discussions naturally have no collective responsibility for the views expressed here but one thing did strike me often in the course of the enquiry : people of diverse political and professional backgrounds who have made some close study of China often agree to a remarkable extent about particular aspects of Chinese politics and strategy; their conclusions, nevertheless, are often remote from the bulk of journalistic or official comment on such matters. Why this should be so would make a study in itself. This essay, however, is not concerned with such second order questions. At the suggestion of the Institute it has been written with the general rather than the specialist reader in mind and seeks to state as clearly as possible what seem to be reasonable conclusions in an area of debate which has often been both turbulent and acrimonious.

Arthur Huck
University of Melbourne

CONTENTS

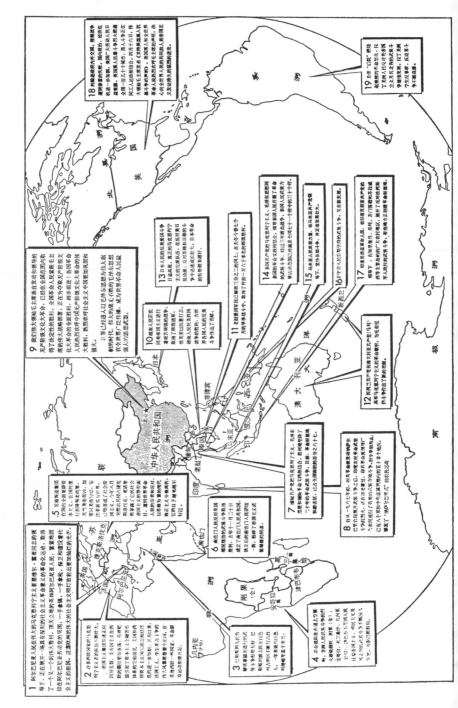

MAP OF THE EXCELLENT WORLD SITUATION

Source: *People's Daily* 26th Sept. 1968

COMMENTARY:

1. The Albanian people led by the great Marxist–Leninist Comrade Enver Hoxha are unfolding a revolutionization movement of profound significance for socialist revolution and have won one great victory after another. The heroic, valiant Albanian people are closely rallied around the Albanian Party of Labour. With pick in one hand and rifle in the other, they are safeguarding and building their socialist motherland. This great beacon of socialism in Europe is shining in ever greater splendour.

2. The ranks of the Marxist–Leninists in many West European countries are growing.

The imperialist bloc is speeding to disintegration. United States imperialism's domination over Western Europe has weakened. Devaluation of sterling has thrown the capitalist monetary system into unprecedented confusion. The political and economic crises of the United States and West European capitalist countries have worsened. Since May the great storm of workers' and students' revolutionary struggle has swept France. In some other West European countries revolutionary mass movements followed in rapid succession.

3. An excellent situation exists in the Palestinian people's armed struggle to liberate their homeland in Israeli-occupied areas the Palestinian guerrillas struck repeated blows at the enemy. In the past year over 5,000 Israeli aggressor troops were killed or wounded.

4. The flames of the African people's armed struggle are raging fiercer. Armed struggle of the peoples of Congo (K), Angola, Mozambique, Guinea (Bissau) and Zimbabwe against imperialism, colonialism and their lackeys are growing in depth and winning new victories.

5. The Soviet revisionist renegade clique has brought about all-round capitalist restoration at home and is pushing a policy of capitulation and betrayal abroad. Acting as United States imperialism's accomplice and stepping up collaboration with it to re-divide the world, it has degenerated into social-imperialism. Its sudden invasion and occupation of Czechoslovakia in August has further exposed its vicious social–imperialist features and has been

9

denounced and opposed by the world's revolutionary people. Modern revisionism headed by Soviet revisionism is crumbling. Each day is harder for it.

6. The South Yemeni people's armed struggle against British colonial rule has triumphed. The People's Republic of Southern Yemen was established on November 30, 1967. An imperialist plot for armed subversion was smashed.

7. Integrating Marxism–Leninism, Mao Tse-tung's thought, with the practice of the Burmese revolution, the Communist Party of Burma has successfully waged twenty years of revolutionary armed struggle. At present revolutionary bases and guerrilla zones cover 67 per cent of the country's area.

8. Since early 1967 when revolutionary Indian Communists mobilized the Naxalbari peasants to launch armed struggle, the flames of the Indian peasants' revolutionary armed struggle has spread rapidly. The revolutionary Indian Communists are leading the broad masses of peasants in heroic armed struggle to seize land. Up to early 1968 'Naxalbari-type' peasant movements had erupted in fifty areas in eight states and regions under direct central control.

9. Initiated and led by our great leader Chairman Mao himself, the great proletarian cultural revolution has won decisive victory throughout China. Closely following Chairman Mao's great strategic plan, China's revolutionary people are forging ahead to seize all-round victory! Revolutionary people of the world hail the splendid victory of China's becoming more consolidated and powerful.

The world has entered the era where Mao Tse-tung's thought is the great banner. The great, invincible thought of Mao Tse-tung is being spread throughout the world and has become the most powerful ideological weapon of the world's revolutionary people.

10. Brilliant victories won by the Vietnamese people in their arduous and resolute war against United States imperialism have contributed to the anti-United States struggle of the peoples.

11. The Laotian patriotic armed forces and people have liberated two-thirds of the country. In seven months of dry season fighting, from last winter to this spring, they won a brilliant victory in wiping out over 16,000 enemies.

12. The New Zealand Communist Party and the Communist Party of Australia (M–L), holding high the revolutionary banner

of Marxism–Leninism, have made new contributions to the struggle against imperialism and revisionism.

13. The Japanese people's anti-United States patriotic struggle is steadily mounting. The ranks of the genuine Marxist–Leninist left are growing rapidly in the struggle against the United States–Japanese reactionaries, Soviet revisionism and Japanese revisionism.

14. The Communist Party of Thailand, integrating Marxism–Leninism, Mao Tse-tung's thought, with the practice of the Thai revolution, is leading the Thai people in revolutionary armed struggle. After three years of guerrilla warfare the Thai people's armed forces are now active in thirty of the country's seventy-one provinces.

15. Led by the Communist Party of Malaya, the Malayan people's armed forces have persisted in protracted struggle and their ranks are growing.

16. There has been a new development of the protracted armed struggle in which the Philippine people have persevered.

17. Led by the Communist Party of Indonesia, revolutionary Indonesian people have launched armed struggle against the fascist military régime in vast rural areas of the main islands of Kalimantan, Java, Sumatra and Sulawesi and are building revolutionary bases in some areas.

18. The Johnson Administration is beset with difficulties at home and abroad. It has suffered severe defeats in its war of aggression against Vietnam. The political and economic crises at home have further sharpened. The broad masses of the working people in the United States are daily awakening. The flames of the Afro-American struggle against tyranny have blazed in more than 100 cities. The Afro-American struggle is now integrating with the workers' movement. On April 16, our great leader Chairman Mao issued his 'Statement in Support of the Afro-American Struggle Against Violent Repression'. Afro-Americans and revolutionary people of the world warmly acclaim Chairman Mao's statement and are resolved to launch a sustained and vigorous offensive against United States imperialism, the common enemy of the world's people.

19. The flames of revolution are raging in United States imperialism's 'backyard'. The Latin American people's armed struggle against United States imperialism and its lackeys continues to develop. The struggle of the Latin American students against tyranny and persecution is steadily expanding.

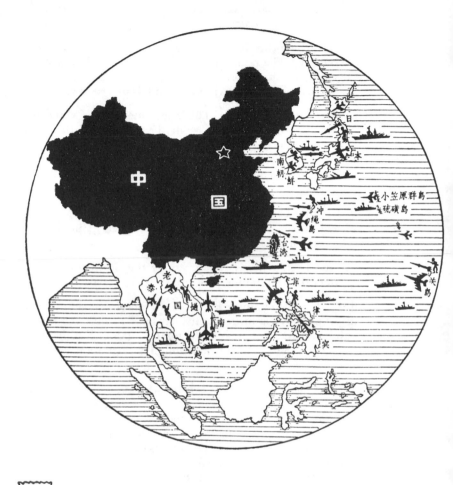

美帝国主义对中国的军事包围（示意图）

钦　哲绘

American Imperialism's Military Encirclement of China

Source: *People's Daily* 29th Jan. 1966

Symbols: 1. United States Troops.　2. Naval Bases.　3. Air bases.
4. Missile Bases.　5. Aircraft Carriers.　6. Nuclear Submarines.

INTRODUCTION

It is a common liberal assumption that greater communication between nations must lead to a lessening of the possibility of conflict between them. This is unfortunately not a self-evident truth. It is at least possible that the more the members of different social systems or different countries discovered about each other the more their antipathies would increase. In the case of China and the outside world there are peculiar difficulties in putting any such assumption to the test. The language barrier is not really the greatest. It does exist but it is not impenetrable. Nor is the 'bamboo curtain' the basic problem. It is probably true that there are fewer foreigners of any sort now living in China than at any time in the last hundred years and certainly few young Chinese born in China now have the opportunity of direct knowledge of any other country. It is also true that diplomatic life for most envoys is severely circumscribed and that numbers of countries, including of course the United States, have no representatives at all in Peking. China nevertheless has not been entirely isolated and numbers of smaller powers have had quite extensive contacts. Australia, for example, a country with a population of only 12 million has no diplomatic relations with the People's Republic but this has not prevented considerable numbers of Australians from visiting China, nor even a few Chinese Communist functionaries from visiting Australia. The Australian visitors have been extremely varied in type. They have included the leaders of the Australian Communist Party (Marxist–Leninist), a small pro-Peking group formed after a split with the main Australian Communist Party; their pronouncements faithfully follow the current Peking line and are regularly cited by Peking. Representatives of the Australian Wheat Board travel regularly to China and private Australian traders frequently attend the mainland trade fairs. Australians have been employed as 'foreign experts' teaching English in Chinese institutions where several of them were

13

strategically placed to observe the Cultural Revolution in action. The Australia–China Society has sponsored tours by groups of teachers and others. Sections of the Chinese Academy of Science have invited Australian academics to visit Chinese institutes. Tours of students have been arranged and until recently it was also possible for individuals to arrange tours through the China Travel Service.

Canadian experience has been very similar and examples from many other countries could be cited. From much of this to-ing and fro-ing very little is learnt. Thousands of peoples have in fact been through this mill since the early 1950s and many of the travellers' reports are wearingly similar. The limitations of state tourism of the Chinese type are obvious. The life of the tourist is very circumscribed. If he is a single traveller he travels in high bourgeois comfort. He may find himself on a crowded train with a whole compartment to himself. Travelling by air he is clearly not surrounded by itinerant peasants. His hotel room will have a bath attached. He will visit historic or scenic spots by car accompanied only by the driver and an interpreter from the travel service. He will eat extremely well and he can drink plentifully as long as he does not want Scotch whisky or French brandy. If he is travelling as a member of an invited group he will be nearly as comfortable. He will probably meet more officials depending on what sort of group he is connected with. If he is a student travelling with a student group he may not be quite so luxuriously treated; he will be expected to show more solidarity with the workers and peasants but not to a painful degree. He will not be able to drive himself around, or hitch-hike or camp.

These limitations have led some students to argue that there is very little value in trying to visit China at all. If travel is so well organized and controlled what is the point of going to all the trouble and expense of following a circuit which so many others have previously followed? More can certainly be learned about China by spending a term in a good library than by travelling there for three weeks but it is surely also true that a reasonably informed traveller can gain some useful impressions of the general condition of a country, however privileged his own position, as long as he spends enough time just looking about him with a moderately objective eye.

For this essay, however, the pertinent question is whether any such impressions are useful or relevant in interpreting Chinese strategic outlooks? My own short visits at the end of 1965 and early in 1966 have undoubtedly influenced the analysis which follows. Discussions with others who have been in the country at later dates during the Cultural Revolution have tended to reinforce my own impressions. It has been interesting to compare notes, for instance, with the Australian students who have travelled in China between 1966 and 1968. Few of them have been political activists or markedly sympathetic to the régime. What they have been is curious and anxious to see for themselves what China is like, and vacation travel schemes have made it possible for many of them to make the trip in groups. For them it has been student tourism but they have nearly always been received as if they formed a delegation. Their student hosts often assumed that they had come to China especially to study the Thought of Mao Tse-tung and they were puzzled to find this was not the case. The Australian students for their part were often astounded not so much by the ignorance of the Chinese about the outside world but by their lack of interest in it. Most of them knew only one thing about Australia, that she had a Marxist–Leninist (pro-Peking) Party led by Comrade Hill, and that was all they wanted to know. For people who were supposed to see themselves now as leaders of world revolution they showed an astonishing lack of interest in the actual conditions of foreign countries. They knew the correct formulae for describing the different countries but they were simply not interested in anything other than the formulae.

Other impressions are equally paradoxical: China appears a country both economically backward and advanced, militant and passive, militarized but not militaristic. However much such seemingly contradictory impressions are drawn on and however many illustrative anecdotes are cited the fact remains that for an understanding of how the Chinese see the problems of national security we have to rely mainly on what the leadership has said and on our observations of their conduct of international affairs. On some questions they remain extremely reticent but generally the problem is not the shortage of information but the extent of the flood of words which pours forth. In this vast ideological sea how are we to discern the important currents? The interpretation of such language is not simply a 'linguistic' matter; the basic difficulty is in discovering how the key symbols are used. No accumulation of data will assist us if we do not understand the Chinese interpretive framework within which the symbols, both familiar and exotic, are made to operate.

This essay is itself an attempt at interpretation. Its validity must be tested by the usual hard test – how useful a guide it is to the course of future events.

Chapter One

CHINESE OUTLOOKS

For more than a hundred years the government of China has been subject to ceaseless strains; not just the normal strains which any administrative system is designed to bear but great stresses which have more than once destroyed the structure. Rebellion, civil war and attacks from European and Asian armies resulted in much fragmentation of the Ch'ing empire and the Republic. No Chinese government in the past century has enjoyed control over all the territory usually regarded as Chinese. The present People's Republic is no exception; it is one party to a stalemated civil war which has poisoned China for forty years and involved her in the most frustrating foreign entanglements. Under such conditions literate Chinese, the people who see themselves as responsible for the preservation of their culture, have been ceaselessly concerned with the problem of national salvation. The common people may often have suffered dumbly, not comprehending the endless miseries which were inflicted upon them, but countless young Chinese have burned with the desire to end the chaos and restore the unity of the great dynasties. It may seem strange that so many of the best of them in this century should have seen in Marxism the road to salvation. Although it appears to be an alien and internationalist creed Marxism can mean a variety of things to different adaptors. It can have intense ethical appeal and it can be reconciled with the most intense nationalism. Indeed the demands of the new Chinese nationalism were met in the most satisfactory way by the Leninist extension of Marxism which made the theory of imperialism the central doctrine. The Sinification of Marxism has now reached the point where Chinese spokesmen insist that only the thought of Chairman Mao truly expresses the great doctrine. Those who acknowledge his genius are true Marxist–Leninists; all others are revisionists or worse.

The irony of this transmutation may be lost on the Academicians of the Soviet Union but is it really so surprising a development? In the eyes of the mandarins the superiority of China has always rested on a superiority of doctrine. Their ancient system of government was not superior simply because the empire was vast, populous and unified; its material strength on the contrary flowed from its virtue and the basis of its virtue was immutable (Confucian) doctrine. Because the Emperor embodied certain immutable moral truths his country was powerful and prosperous. Indeed if the condition of the country worsened and the populace suffered this was a sign that the Emperor had abandoned the path of virtue and forfeited the heavenly mandate. The basis of all superiority was moral superiority founded on true doctrine. Representatives of foreign potentates who arrived bearing tribute were supposed to be showing their recognition of this fact and therefore of the Emperor's superior place in the scheme of things.

The question of how the Chinese view their place in the world is a problem often posed by foreigners. Even now most Chinese would probably be puzzled by it. They would not know how to answer it in the first place because it had never crossed their minds. In the past the question simply did not arise. China was not seen as one country so placed geographically that many other countries were contiguous to it. China was the world, peopled by the Han, a black-haired people whose civilization defined the limits of the world. Other peoples were recognized to exist but they were simply outsiders, people of inferior culture. There have been many peoples and many states in the history of the world who have been convinced of the superiority of their culture and their race but none perhaps has preserved the conviction with such persistence or, possibly, with such justification. Even if we discount the legendary past and make every allowance for the discontinuity of dynasties and the periods of internal turmoil China preserved a civic culture for a longer period and at a higher level than any other in Asia. Her more accessible neighbours, in particular the Japanese, the Koreans and the Vietnamese, have drawn heavily on it over centuries.

It was a superiority which appeared obvious to all. Even the illiterate knew that the Empire was vast, that beyond the confines of the village there were many millions of Han. Isolated villagers knew that the great district officials whom they feared represented the distant power of the Emperor and the great unity of the state. The literate classes rejoiced in the self-sufficiency of the empire, the fact that it produced everything it wanted, needed nothing from outside barbarians. Their official histories idealized the virtues of its imperial and bureacratic system of government and repeated the great self-evident truths of the official philosophy. The basis of the social order was a true appreciation of one's station and its duties; the due subordination of children to parents, wives to husbands, officials to Emperor. Virtuous officials, selected for their intelligence and orthodoxy, were the guardians of the immutable social order. The written language, complex and non-phonetic, reinforced in the élite the conviction of immemorial rectitude and imperturbable ability to deal with any problem of government or manners.

The foreign invasions of the nineteenth century produced a profound cultural shock. Here were people armed with a new technology who could not be dealt with by the traditional methods. They would not act as tribute bearers nor recognize, however symbolically, the superiority of the Emperor and his Empire. Pitting one of them against the others had only limited success; they were quite likely in a crisis to combine with the joint object of extracting further concessions from China to their mutual advantage. They could not be kept at a distance and handled successfully by the provincial authorities. They demanded central representation and recognition as powers equal to China. Until late in the nineteenth century there was no bureaucratic machinery in Peking for dealing with foreigners or foreign governments on any basis of equality or reciprocity. China sent no ambassadors abroad and was reluctant to accept the diplomatic conventions which the European states had developed in recent centuries for handling formal relations among themselves. It was obvious to the mandarinate that European conventions presupposed a system of national states, not equal in power, but theoretically at least equal in diplomatic standing, with defined territories and separate centres of allegiance which in every way conflicted with the traditional Chinese view.

The Chinese have been obsessively concerned with their humiliations in the nineteenth century. All levels of society appeared to be affected. The presence of gunboats and soldiers demonstrated to all the inability of the imperial house to protect its subjects. The evidence of new machines and manufactured goods revealed the disparity of wealth between the new states of the West and the old agricultural civilizations of the East. The populace deeply resented the very presence of the foreigners and outbursts of violent xenophobic hatred were not uncommon. Among the literate, however, there was an even more profound malaise. The Western incursions, Western manners, Western dogmatism and confidence had challenged their belief in the moral basis of their civic culture. Arguments raged for decades over what should be done to meet the challenge. Some argued that only superficial changes needed to be made; if the Western technical skills were acquired, in particular the military skills and equipment, the foreigners could be hurled out and China could continue on the basis of her unchanging principles.

Conservatives argued for a strengthening of every traditional institution and a most cautious approach to innovation. More and more, however, the younger *literati* argued for revolutionary change. The old order had been discredited and a new must be found. In typical Chinese style, however, comparatively little attention was given to what political institutions should be developed to replace the old. The great thing was to find a new system of belief, a new philosophy which could replace outworn Confucianism.

The new Leninist doctrine on the nature of imperialism could not have fallen into more receptive hands. Here was not only a convincing explanation of what had happened to China but a doctrine of certain hope for the future. The woes of China could all be confidently credited to the effects of capitalism but it was a capitalism on its last legs – the highest stage of capitalism was also the stage of its farewell appearance; the monster had feet of clay. Whatever the metaphors the message was clear. What Lenin actually wrote about imperialism was of little importance and probably little read. What mattered was the hopefulness of the new doctrine. It is interesting to compare Lenin's own 1917 tract *Imperialism, the Highest Stage of Capitalism* with any of Mao's writings on imperialism, the compilation, for example put out by the editorial department of the *People's Daily* in 1958, *Imperialism and All Reactionaries are Paper Tigers*. The great bulk of Lenin's essay is taken up with economic analysis of the state of capitalism in the late nineteenth and early twentieth centuries, and how this can be squared with Marxist predictions. Monopoly capitalism is seen as necessarily resulting in war. 'Imperialism' is defined as 'moribund capitalism'. Mao's writing, however, is almost devoid of economic analysis. His style is heroic and romantic, confidently boosting popular morale. The Chinese people are threatened by imperialism but in the long run they will triumph. No weapons, atomic or otherwise, can in the end defeat the revolutionary masses. The content of the original doctrine becomes of little importance compared with the functions it can be called upon to perform in a Chinese setting. Such utilization of foreign doctrine has not been confined to Communists. Extreme nationalists like Chiang Kai-shek have been even more adept at manipulating the theory of imperialism so that it becomes a way of placing the responsibility for China's modern woes on to the hated activities of foreigners.

In *China's Destiny* he described at length how the imperialists had over the past century intruded into all spheres of Chinese life. They had consolidated their gains at China's expense in many 'unequal' treaties and these had become the chief source of evil in modern China. The combined political, economic, social, ethical and psychological effects of the treaties had, in Chiang's view, been disastrous; only their complete abrogation and a return to traditional Chinese virtues could ensure the salvation of the nation. He was particularly suspicious of those Chinese who advocated foreign political theories either liberal or Communist. 'As for the struggle between Liberalism and Communism,' he wrote, without giving any specific historical reference, 'it was merely a reflection of the opposition of Anglo–American theories to those of Soviet Russia. Not only were such political theories unsuited to the national economy and the people's livelihood, and opposed to the spirit of China's own civilization, but also the people that promoted them forgot that they were Chinese and that they should study and apply foreign theories for the benefit of China. As a result, their copying of Western theories only caused the decay and ruin of Chinese civilization, and made it easy for the imperialists to carry on cultural aggression.'[1]

In the case of Mao there has been a great deal of rather rabbinical argument among Western sinologues as to the degree of originality in his contributions to the storehouse of Marxism–Leninism. Such arguments seem unimportant to most Chinese:

[1] Chiang Kai-shek, *China's Destiny* (New York: Roy Publishers, 1947), p. 100.

the great thinker is not necessarily a great innovator but a great exponent of universal truth. Dialectical materialism is seen as the great truth, providing the universe of discourse. Once that is established it can, paradoxically, be almost ignored. The important question becomes its application, what it means in the 'concrete conditions of the Chinese Revolution' and the world revolutionary situation. The Chinese significantly do not talk about 'Mao-*ism*' (*chu-i*) but incessantly about Mao's 'thought', his *ssu-hsiang*, the application of the metaphysic to the real. Soviet theoreticians may complain that the thought has moved further and further from what they see as practical applications of Marxism but this complaint in Chinese eyes only proves their revisionist blindness. Chinese publications in recent years have insisted that the Thought of Mao Tse-tung is the real light of the world. In language which no traditional defender of Chinese superiority could have outdone they have lauded the universal significance of his utterance. They are quite aware of the fact that most of the governments of the world do not share this enthusiasm but this is perfectly explicable to them : they see most of the governments of the world as self-perpetuating cliques, divorced from the masses and representing at best the interests of a narrowly-based class. The masses of the world, however, cannot be deceived for ever and Chinese publicists constantly produce evidence of how the masses have seen through the distortions of reactionary propaganda and have made a real estimate of the trend of events in the world.

How does the world look from Peking at the high-water mark of the Maoist era? In 1968 the *People's Daily* twice presented annotated maps of the 'Excellent World Situation'. Both projections showed China roughly in the middle, a little left of centre, flanked by Europe and Africa on one side and the Americas on the other.

The only city marked is Peking, where, according to the map of 26 September, 'initiated and led by our great leader Chairman Mao himself, the great proletarian cultural revolution has won decisive victory throughout China. Closely following Chairman Mao's great strategic plan, China's revolutionary people are forging ahead to seize all-round victory ! Revolutionary people of the world hail the splendid victory of China's great cultural revolution and socialist China's becoming more consolidated and powerful.

CHINESE OUTLOOKS

'The world has entered the era where Mao Tse-tung's thought is the great banner. The great invincible thought of Mao Tse-tung is being spread throughout the world and has become the most powerful ideological weapon of the world's revolutionary people.'

(The earlier map of 1 January similarly referred to socialist China as the 'centre of world revolution' and an additional box recorded that the successful explosion of the country's first hydrogen bomb had greatly uplifted the morale of the world's revolutionary people. There was also a reference to the serious blows dealt to British imperialism in Hong Kong, a matter not referred to in the September map.) The Albanian box is given pride of place in the top left corner. 'This great beacon of socialism in Europe is shining in ever greater splendour.'

In the rest of Europe 'the ranks of Marxist–Leninists in many West European countries are growing'.

Excellent revolutionary conditions are reported in twelve other areas of the world: Palestine, Angola, the Yemen, India, Burma, Vietnam, Laos, Thailand, Malaya, the Philippines, Indonesia and Latin America. (For details see the map on page 8). In Oceania 'The New Zealand Communist Party and the Communist Party of Australia (Marxist–Leninist), holding high the revolutionary banner of Marxism–Leninism, have made new contributions to the struggle against imperialism and revisionism'. In the Soviet Union, on the other hand, 'the Soviet revisionist renegade clique has brought about all-round capitalist restoration at home and is pushing a policy of capitulation and betrayal abroad. Acting as United States imperialism's accomplice and stepping up collaboration with it to redivide the world, it has degenerated into social-imperialism. Its sudden invasion and occupation of Czechoslovakia in August has further exposed its vicious social-imperialist features and has been denounced and opposed by the world's revolutionary people. Modern revisionism, headed by Soviet revisionism, is crumbling. Each day is harder for it.'

The United States, as might be expected, is in a bad way, 'beset with difficulties at home and abroad. . . . On April 16 our great leader Chairman Mao, issued his "Statement in Support of the Afro-American Struggle Against Violent Repression". Afro-American and revolutionary people of the world warmly acclaim

23

Chairman Mao's statement and are resolved to launch a sustained and vigorous offensive against United States imperialism, the common enemy of the world's people.'

The observations are so highly selective that the construction of the whole map takes on the appearance of ritual, a special performance in accord with the official philosophy of how the world is going. If there are no events which can be presented as showing the appropriate trend then the trend is simply said to exist, as in the Australian and New Zealand box which has been quoted or the similar reference to the Philippines : 'there has been a new development of the protracted armed struggle in which the Philippine people have persevered.' To say that such a performance is ritualistic is not the same as saying it is one of self-deception. The publicists are perfectly aware that there are countervailing tendencies in the world. The official philosophy indeed specifically allows for them in terms of a universal doctrine of contradiction. The selection of favourable portents is an exercise in reassurance, a declaration of faith.

Different political cultures have different types of ritual performance; what goes down well in the White House does not necessarily go down well in Whitehall. In either place intelligent observers rapidly learn to distinguish ritual utterance from statements of specific policy; the two things may be only remotely related. In highly ritualistic cultures like the Chinese it is more than ever important not to interpret ritualistic utterances as planning statements.

It would be absurd to argue that the Maoist rulers of China see the world in exactly the same way as the imperial mandarinate of earlier centuries but their political styles look increasingly alike : China is the source of all wisdom and correct political ideas. The content of the wisdom is, of course, very different. The old mandarinate was characterized by enormous complacency, the new by a basic insecurity which has been rationalized in an ideology of change. The old envisaged a permanent world order, essentially unchanging, the new envisages continual change. However, the concepts of a world order are in both cases primarily doctrinal. This is not to say that they are or were remote from any political reality. A doctrine must have *some* relation to reality if it is to function at all, but the relationship may be somewhat oblique. The traditional doctrine bore some relation to the reali-

24

ties of Chinese foreign relations during the Ch'ing dynasty, but not much. Similarly, Maoist doctrine bears some relation to the modern world : much of the world is in a transitional stage; many of the new states are unstable creations carved out of dead empires; many do have high revolutionary potential. In both cases, however, it would be naïve to draw from such doctrinaire pictures of the world direct inferences about what Chinese policy would be in any specific case.

In the traditional view China lay at the centre of a basically stable world. The stability was not to be achieved by means of a balance of power as that idea has been understood in Europe. Indeed, the notion of a balance of power is essentially a European one, presupposing a system of nation-states with clearly defined boundaries, independent sovereign governments and equality of status. Stability in the Chinese view depended rather on the recognition of a natural order which corresponded roughly to the actual situation of Imperial China in her heyday. The heartland, the traditional Eighteen Provinces, was the seat of Han civilization. Beyond this, in roughly concentric zones, lay regions of different importance and interest to China. The contiguous non-Han regions of Korea, Manchuria, Mongolia, Chinese Turkestan, Tibet and Annam were clearly of the greatest importance. If these could not be brought under direct Chinese control they must at least accept some sort of Chinese suzerainty. On occasions of course the tables were turned and alien conquest dynasties like the Mongol and the Manchu dominated the Chinese heartland. The Ch'ing (Manchu) dynasty at its greatest extent regarded some areas like Mongolia as more or less incorporated territories, others, more distant, as tributary regions. The celebrated tribute system, whatever else it may have been, was certainly not a colonial system as that term has been understood in the West.

It was indeed hardly an administrative system at all but rather a set of rituals by which 'non-Chinese rulers participated in the Chinese world order by observing the appropriate forms and ceremonies (li) in their contact with the Son of Heaven. Taken together, these practices constituted the tribute system.'[2] Fairbank has summarized its regulations in the Ch'ing period as follows:

[2] J. K. Fairbank (ed.), *The Chinese World Order: Traditional China's Foreign Relations* (Cambridge, Mass.: Harvard University Press, 1968), p. 10.

(a) non-Chinese rulers were given a patent of appointment and an official seal for use in correspondence;

(b) they were given a noble rank in the Ch'ing hierarchy;

(c) they dated their communications by the Ch'ing calendar, that is, by the Ta Ch'ing reign-title;

(a) they presented tribute memorials of various sorts on appropriate statuary occasions;

(e) they also presented a symbolic tribute (kung) of local products;

(f) they or their envoys were escorted to court by imperial post;

(g) they performed the appropriate ceremonies of the Ch'ing court, notably the kotow;

(h) they received imperial gifts in return; and

(i) they were granted certain privileges at the frontier and at the capital.[3]

Missions continued to be recorded in China throughout the declining years of the Ching dynasty. Between 1840 and 1894 there were no less than 46 tribute missions from Korea; missions arrived from Siam until 1853, from Burma until 1875, from Vietnam until 1883 and the last one from Nepal arrived in 1908.[4]

China indeed has never had overseas colonies or any overseas empire comparable to the great eighteenth and nineteenth century European colonial empires. The countries which sent tribute often used the occasion of the tribute mission simply to facilitate trading relations. They made formal acknowledgement of the Chinese Emperor's superior position but in most cases their domestic political arrangements were very little influenced by the formalities.

This traditional Chinese view of a world order with China as its natural centre has been often enough described but how far it has had a continuing influence on how modern Chinese see the world has been hotly debated. Educated Chinese have come to terms with the idea of China as a modern nation-state in a world of nation-states but this has left unresolved the question of what constituted the territory of the modern Chinese state. The extent of the traditional area where China expected to have at least a

[3] Fairbank, op. cit. pp. 10–11.
[4] Fairbank, op. cit. pp. 265–66.

formal primary position had been fairly well understood even if much of it had had no exact boundaries. Reference books published under both the Nationalists and the Communists have indicated it with some precision in maps.[5] Although some variations occur these maps generally include within the 'Chinese' area Sakhalin, Korea, Formosa, most of British Borneo and the Sulu Archipelago, all of mainland South-East Asia, Assam, the Himalayan Kingdoms, Tibet, much of Soviet Middle Asia, Chinese Turkestan, all of Mongolia and part of the Soviet Far East. Beyond this lay what Ginsberg has called an Outer Asian Zone – Persia, India, Indonesia, the Philippines, Japan – countries relatively well known to the Chinese. Beyond that again lay all the rest of the world, 'in Chinese eyes largely undifferentiated'.[6] It is often suggested that many Chinese still see the world essentially in terms of this model: a central China, an Asian periphery and an alien beyond. It is one thing however to assert that traditional models can have a long persistent effect on patterns of thought and quite another to suggest that they have a dominant influence on policy making. Nationalist and Communist alike have talked of their 'lost' territories, by which they have meant the large peripheral segments of the zone of primary Chinese concern which were detached by different imperial countries during the decline of the Ch'ing dynasty. The list of intrusions is formidable : Russia into her new Far East and Outer Mongolia, Japan into Korea, Formosa and later Manchuria and China herself, France into Indo-China, Britain into Burma and so on.

It does not follow that any modern Chinese state will want to regain all these 'lost' territories in the sense of incorporating them in a new Chinese Empire (whether Communist or not). Some of these territories were never formally administered by China and they certainly did not lie within a precisely defined Chinese boundary whatever modern maps may show. The traditional Chinese state at many points did not have precise boundaries. It faded

[5] See the composite map in Alastair Lamb, *Asian Frontiers Studies in a Continuing Problem* (Melbourne: F. W. Cheshire, 1968), p. 30, which is drawn from maps dated 1925 and 1954. Compare the map in Norton Ginsberg 'On the Chinese Perception of a World Order', in Tang Tsou (ed.), *China in Crisis* (Vol. II) (Chicago: Chicago University Press, 1968), p. 77.

[6] Ginsberg, *op. cit*, p. 79.

away into areas of less and less concern to China until the Great Unknown was reached. The problem for any modern Chinese state is precisely to determine some practicable boundaries. In the early nineteenth century there was no such thing as the internationally recognized boundary of China and the Chinese were not interested in such a concept. The re-establishment of something like the old order, however, would clearly be incompatible with the establishment of a modern nation-state. The first thing a modern state has to have is a clearly defined boundary, widely recognized, delimited on maps and demarcated, that is marked out on the ground, where possible. The establishment of such a boundary has not been an easy task for either Republican or Communist China and, where it has been agreed on, the problems of relations with the many different states on the other side of it have not disappeared.

On the face of it the Maoist picture of the world in revolutionary ferment is the antithesis of the traditional Chinese view of a stable world order with China at its centre. The two views are not however particularly difficult to reconcile. Both have a determined interest in removing alien (distant, foreign, 'imperialist') influence from the periphery of China. Traditionalists could see the successful accomplishment of this as the re-establishment of the old conditions for a secure China, revolutionaries as a set-back for the imperialists which strengthened the forces of Marxism–Leninism. In both cases, however, these guiding pictures should not be taken as identical with concrete policies: from a map which shows China as the centre of world revolutionary thought it does not allow that fomenting revolution will be the prime Chinese object in all dealings with foreign states; from a map showing 'lost' territories it does not follow that a modern Chinese state must be hell-bent on 'regaining' them in the sense of including them within a territorial border which did not clearly exist before they were 'lost'.

Chapter Two

THREATS TO CHINA

The official rhetoric of both Nationalists in the Republican era and Communists before and after 1949 has been dominated by the picture of a threatened China. The threat comes from imperialists of all sorts, that is non-Han people who have moved into areas adjacent to China or invaded China proper either militarily, economically or culturally. A great deal of emotion has been poured into denunciation of the imperialists and ritualized expressions of hostility figure prominently in official statements. Communist name-calling combines old and new images and covers a very wide range. United States Imperialism 'will never lay down its butcher's knife and will never become a Buddha'. The social-imperialists in the Kremlin are 'the New Tsars' who 'can never cover up their hideous features'. The menacing activities of the imperialists and their henchmen are dwelt on incessantly but just as regularly their defeat is said to be certain. Imperialists are dangerous and threatening but they are also Paper Tigers.

'Commentator's' views on British withdrawal from the Far East follow exactly this 'dialectical' pattern: 'British Imperialism' is 'On Its Last Legs', according to the translation in *Peking Review* (26 January 1968) but 'of course, British imperialism's troop withdrawal does not in the least mean it will from now on lay down its butcher's knife and become a Buddha. On the contrary, this is actually a retreat in preparation for advancing later . . . a step to realize its dream of restoring the British Empire some time in the future.' On the other hand, 'all the efforts of British imperialism to save itself from its doom will be nothing but a desperate last-ditch struggle'. There is an important logical consequence of this type of arguing which is perhaps not widely understood; no policy conclusions whatever can be drawn from it. Maoist theses like 'Imperialism and all reactionaries are Paper Tigers' are strictly incorrigible, that is, they cannot be falsified

29

by reference to any set of facts. If the imperialists are not acting very much like paper tigers at the moment this does not matter; in the long run their weaknesses will reveal themselves. If the British appear to be giving their empire away they are still imperialists at heart. If statements like this are incorrigible, that is to say, held to be true no matter what actually happens, it follows that they have no predictive value; they cannot tell you what to expect at any particular time because they are consistent with anything happening. They are therefore of no value as specific guides to action; they do not indicate what ought to be done in any particular case. Equally they are of no value to outsiders anxious to know how the Chinese will react in any particular situation. This is not to say they are entirely pointless or have no function. Clearly they legitimize in some degree a very pervasive distrust which some analysts see as a dominant characteristic of Chinese political culture. They also act as a type of high level morale booster, an up-to-date equivalent of hanging out more flags. The idea, however, that by a study of Maoist ideological writing alone we can obtain an accurate indication of Chinese plans and intentions and a precise guide to what their future policies will be is not only naïve but dangerous.

Chinese tend to be acutely conscious of the differences which often exist between social realities and the ritual formulae used to describe them. This does not mean they decry ritual expression. On the contrary, the greatest importance is attached to correct expression. In a dangerous world ritual produces a semblance of order and provides the consolations of certainty. Only the very innocent, however, imagine that in the tiger world of politics rational decisions can be made simply by invoking the appropriate formulae. As Lucien Pye has observed, with the Chinese 'emotions are not usually closely geared to action, and the former do not generally mirror the latter. Action can occur with few clues about the submerged feelings and the sudden expression of emotion does not provide a reliable guide for predicting behaviour.'[1] How significant then is the constant repetition of the rhetoric of a threatened China?

Visitors to China do not gain an impression of a highly militarized country much concerned with problems of defence. Some

[1] Lucien Pye, *The Spirit of Chinese Politics* (Cambridge, Mass.: MIT Press, 1968), p. 101.

of the reasons for this are obvious: most of the soldiers in China are stationed in places where visitors are not taken. Another reason is less obvious : the level of forces, considering the size of the country and the size of the population, is in reality rather low. On paper the numbers in the People's Liberation Army, the generic term for all the armed forces, seem huge – some 2,761,000 men (including railway engineer troops), but this figure is much smaller than the numbers in the regular armed forces of the USSR and smaller again than the numbers in the regular forces of the United States (3,500,000). The disproportion is even more striking if the different sizes of the populations are taken into account: the proportion of men of military age who are actually in the forces is more than three times greater in the Soviet Union than in China and more than four times greater in the United States than in China.[2]

In the countryside it is hard for the bourgeois tourist to find evidence of a preoccupation with the danger of war. Soldiers can be seen near railway bridges but one can travel for hundreds of miles and never see a uniform. As with so many things in China regional differences are often very striking. In Canton the Vietnam war has been, and has been felt to be, very close. Theatrical performances in the parks regularly mimed the shooting down of American aircraft and the capture of American pilots. Ballets extolled the mobility of the Vietnamese guerrillas and their identity with the people. Posters showed the people of the world, of all races, shoulder to shoulder facing the imperialists. In early 1966 a hardworking, intelligent functionary in the Travel Service asked, 'Have you any criticisms to make of the theatrical performances?' To the counter question, 'Why, is there so much emphasis on war?' The answer was emphatic : 'You must understand that we are surrounded: in front the American Imperialists, behind the Soviet Revisionists. We must be prepared for anything.' He was incisive, voluble, but well instructed. He knew the line, but he did not talk as if it were just the line; he sounded as if he was convinced by what he was saying. Farther north, in February 1966, the real war seemed farther away. In a Shanghai Children's Palace the children played on a mock guerrilla training course – tunnels and makeshift bridges, obstacles and hazards – in the garden. Inside they could make model aeroplanes or throw balls

[2] See *The Military Balance 1968–69* (London: ISS, 1968), p. 57.

at effigies of American Presidents – a good hit on Truman and lights lit up. It all seemed much more a game. In Peking the visual evidence of a preoccupation with war and the danger of war seemed even slighter. It was even possible to find a theatre, popular with diplomatic children, where the programme seemed practically devoid of political or military content – jugglers, magicians, tumblers, comedians. Only one item was suddenly reminiscent of Canton : an ᵢimitator produced a nerve-racking imitation of the approach of a bomber, its dive and ultimately its destruction. There was polite applause.

Since then of course much of the Peking cultural establishment has been overturned. The army has much greater control over the arts and entertainment, and there is a more general emphasis on military themes. The heavy guiding hand of Chiang Ching (Madame Mao) has been felt in all spheres. It is frequently said that the Great Proletarian Cultural Revolution has resulted in the army playing a much greater role in non-military affairs than it had in the past. Certainly students touring at the beginning of 1968 came across more soldiers in the cities than they had at the beginning of 1967. No longer did they meet cheerful groups of Red Guards themselves touring the country 'exchanging revolutionary experiences'. Most of the soldiers admittedly were unarmed but this made their non-military roles even more obvious.

It has of course been Maoist orthodoxy for many years that soldiers should not take a narrowly military view of their role in society. The model soldier should identify himself with the people and particularly with the peasantry. He should help them in their tasks whenever he can and should be a model of unselfishness, frugality and morality. Most of the soldiers probably do not find this injunction to merge with the peasantry particularly strange. Most of them after all have peasant backgrounds and expect to return to their native villages after their period of military service. Hence one of the paradoxes of Maoism. Mao is often presented as a man dominated by romantic military models and metaphors, and so perhaps he is, but he has also been consistently opposed to the emergence of professional militarists and militarism. The doctrine of the inseparability of war and politics has often seemed alarming to Westerners but it necessarily has two aspects: not only the militarization of politics, which seems so dangerous, but also the politicization of war which may be quite salutary. That is, no

Maoist should ever forget that strategy is not just a matter of the exercise of military force but must be concerned with the political objectives which may rationally be achieved by the use of force. The dominant Western tradition has emphasized the necessity of the separation of military from political affairs; this has been seen as essential for the preservation of civil primacy and the prevention of military take-overs. The development of military professionalism has further encouraged the idea that most military problems have technical solutions; statesmen may define political goals but generals must rule on their military feasibility. Such a simple dichotomy has been remote from the realities of modern civil and military relationships. As warfare has become more complex and the degree of social involvement in a major conflict has become total the very distinction of 'civil' and 'military' has become blurred. It has become harder and harder to maintain the traditional separation of military and civilian roles.

Mao himself is often presented in popular Western polemics as very crude advocate of *realpolitik*. His most widely known saying is 'Political power grows out of the barrel of a gun,' but the original context of this remark is not often considered by those who quote it. In 1938 the Chinese Communists were faced with the problems of both the civil war against the Kuomintang and the war against the Japanese invaders. A Communist Party which in these circumstances did not concentrate on military affairs was obviously doomed to extinction. 'Communists', Mao wrote, 'do not fight for personal military power but they must fight for military power for the Party, for military power for the people. As a national war of resistance is going on, we must also fight for military power for the nation. Where there is naïvety on the question of military power, nothing whatever can be achieved. It is very difficult for the labouring people, who have been deceived and intimidated by the reactionary ruling classes for thousands of years, to awaken to the importance of having guns in their own hands. Now that Japanese imperialist oppression and the nation-wide resistance to it have pushed our labouring people into the arena of war, Communists should prove themselves the most politically conscious leaders in this war. Every Communist must grasp the truth, "Political power grows out of the barrel of a gun." Our principle is that the Party commands the gun, and the gun must never be allowed to command the Party. Yet, having guns, we can create Party organizations, as witness the powerful Party organizations which the Eighth Route Army has created in northern China. We can also create cadres, create schools, create culture, create mass movements. Everything in Yenan has been created by having guns. All things grow out of the barrel of a gun. According to the Marxist theory of the state, the army is the chief component of state power. Whoever wants to seize and retain state power must have a strong army. Some people ridicule us as advocates of the "omnipotence of war". Yes, we are advocates of the omnipotence of revolutionary war; that is good, not bad, it is Marxist.'[3]

Eleven years later, with victory in sight, Mao could write, in commemoration of the twenty-eighth anniversary of the Party:

'As everyone knows, our Party passed through these twenty-eight years not in peace but amid hardships, for we had to fight enemies, both foreign and domestic, both inside and outside the Party. We thank Marx, Engels, Lenin and Stalin for giving us a weapon. This weapon is not a machine-gun, but Marxism–Leninism.'[4]

In Mao's view any apparent contradiction here is not a cause for concern; it is simply in the nature of things. All things in some sense contain their opposites: to reflect reality all thought must be 'dialectical'. The alleged logic of this is not important but it does have important consequences in Maoist practice: no military problem is ever seen in isolation; there is no such thing in fact as a purely military problem.

Is it possible to discover how the Chinese really assess their politico-military position and what their consequent strategies are likely to be? Many people would be inclined to be pessimistic about the prospects. It needed no Communist revolution to reinforce the addiction to secrecy of the Chinese bureaucrat. The Communist system, however, has its own peculiar ways of airing matters of great public importance. From the plethora of words accompanying the Sino–Soviet dispute and the Cultural Revolution it is possible to construct in some degree a picture of the

[3] Mao Tse-tung, 'Problems of War and Strategy', *Selected Works*, Vol. II (Peking: Foreign Language Publishing House, 1965), pp. 224–25.
[4] Mao Tse-tung, 'On the People's Democratic Dictatorship', *Selected Works*, Vol. IV (Peking: Foreign Language Publishing House, 1961), p. 412.

policy conflicts which have produced so much bitterness and the assessments on which they have been based. Internal polemics thus throw some light on basic preoccupations. Some informative sources are also generally available which were not intended to be.[5] In the various disputes the more rational policies may not always have prevailed, but with some risk of over-generalizing, it does seem possible to discern the main guidelines of the decision makers.

A highly realistic judgement of China's multiple weaknesses would appear to be the most consistently held view of her policy-makers. The existence of fundamental weaknesses has sometimes been admitted, often not, but the Chinese have certainly not made the mistake of so many others in vastly overestimating their strength.

Although there have been disputes on the matter it seems to be understood that the sheer size of the Chinese population is not in itself a source of strength. China has the largest population of any nation on earth but this does not make her the greatest world power any more than India's 520,000,000 make her the second greatest power. There have been Chinese like Sun Yat-sen who have thought that there were not enough Chinese and that they were in danger of being swamped by the hordes of Europe but Chinese economists are mostly more realistic. It is true that economists who argued that the population was expanding faster than the economy and that there simply would not be enough city jobs for the young were attacked as 'Malthusians'. Nevertheless, severe limitation of family size is now official policy, late marriage and birth control are universally urged (and regular attempts are made to draft young city dwellers to the countryside). Mao's own view is supposed to be that on the whole the large population of China is a good thing although it has its problems – a typical Maoist utterance which can be made to cover all eventualities. He told Edgar Snow in early 1965 that he doubted if the population could be 680 to 690 million as some people said.[6] It is possible that there has been more success with the problem of reducing the rate of population growth than most observers thought likely

[5] See discussion of the *Kung-tso T'ung-hsun* (Bulletin of Activities) of the PLA (People's Liberation Army) in the *China Quarterly*, No 18, April–June 1964.

[6] See Edgar Snow, 'Interview with Mao', *New Public*, 27 February 1965.

but no one can be certain about it. The publication of provincial figures during the Cultural Revolution gives some grounds for thinking that the population in mid-1968 might be of the order of 710 million, some 70 million less than common outside estimates. Even if the population is increasing at a rate as low as 1·4 per cent a year, however, the annual increase in food required is enormous. The youthfulness of the population is an even more intractable problem; a more literate young population means a rising demand for satisfying work which is very hard to meet. It is of course maintained that a socialist economy can cope with all such problems, that indeed they are only problems for capitalist economies, but once that has been said the bureaucracy still has to struggle to solve them.

The problem is not one of sheer space. Despite the huge numbers he knows live there, the traveller in China often feels that it is a rather empty country.[7] Many parts of Europe are more densely populated than many parts of China but the bare figures can be misleading. Great areas of China are either too mountainous or too infertile to support large agricultural populations. Extensive internal colonization, however, has occurred since 1949. The minority regions of Inner Mongolia, Sinkiang and Tibet have received very large increases in Han (Chinese) population. Whole new industrial complexes have been developed in the North-West where for centuries the population has been sparse. There is little doubt that with a greatly expanded industrial base and a modernized agriculture China could successfully support an even larger population.

The Chinese economy however is still very weak and is not likely to make really rapid progress. This is not due so much to

[7] Simple territorial expansion by China would not in itself solve the problems presented by a very large population. China has enough desert, jungle and mountainous areas of her own without casting covetous eyes on those of her neighbours. Not all the contiguous territory is as unattractive as the Mongolian deserts but where, further afield, it is fertile, it tends to be densely populated already. The absorption or extermination of millions of Vietnamese, Thais, Burmese or Indians for the sake of extra *lebensraum* is not likely to be seen a very feasible policy to any Chinese government (ignoring altogether the military and political costs). At the most obvious point of expansion, from Kwangsi into Tonkin, China is faced by a people, the Vietnamese, who have a long tradition of bitter opposition to just such a move. The peculiarities of the Sino–Soviet position will be considered later.

any particularly doctrinaire application of Communist economic policy as to the scale and intractability of the problems facing it. Eight out of ten Chinese are still peasants; agriculture is still comparatively backward and the vast peasant economy cannot rapidly be transformed. The modern sector of the industrial economy can perform impressively but it is comparatively limited in size. The transport system of the country is very inadequate for an advanced economy, the railway system far from modern, civil air transport minimal and despite many extensions to roads in border regions a national highway system is almost nonexistent. Communist performance in the direction and modernization of the economy is naturally a highly controversial subject. Most Western economists were impressed with early successes in restoring a war-shattered economy, stabilizing the currency and launching further industrialization. Most Western economists were equally unimpressed with the Great Leap Forward, the Commune Programme, and attempts to force the pace of socialization. Since then the Chinese have been extremely reticent about the detailed state of the economy and have published very few statistics on it. Economists have had to piece together a picture from trade figures and inadequate estimates. The Great Proletarian Cultural Revolution does not seem to have had the disastrous effect on the economy which many predicted but its recent rate of growth does not seem very startling. There seems to be general agreement that the problems facing an economy like China's will not disappear overnight. China is not likely to 'overtake' the advanced countries in the foreseeable future : indeed the gap between the advanced economies and those struggling with modernization is likely to increase.

The present state of the armed forces of China in many ways reflects the weaknesses of the country and the unevenness of her development. On paper the sheer numbers sound very formidable but the closer they are examined the more the deficiencies appear. There are about three million people in the regular and para-military forces in China. (As already mentioned this is considerably less than the totals in either the Soviet Union or the United States). Most of the three million are in land forces. There are only 100,000 in the air force and 136,000 in the navy.[8] The air force with perhaps 2,500 aircraft appears formidable but most of

[8] *The Military Balance 1968–69* (London: ISS), pp. 10–11.

37

its planes are obsolescent. They include no long-range bombers, about 150 11-28 light bombers and a few Tu-4 medium bombers, (these last are copies of the B-29 and became operational in 1946). Most of the fighters are early model MiGs. The air transport fleet has a very limited air-lift capacity. The navy has about 1,000 ships, mostly small patrol and torpedo boats.[9] Most of the larger ships are old as are most of the submarines. There are no aircraft carriers but some 500 shore-based naval aircraft. The army has about 2,500,000 men, some 1,600,000 of them in about 115 line divisions. Of these only four are armoured divisions. Most of the others are comparatively lightly equipped infantry divisions. Many men are in construction and railway units and other support services. An additional 300,000 are in security and border units.

It may seem paradoxical to describe forces of such size as comparatively weak but in terms of a capacity for sustained offensive operations far beyond China's borders they certainly are,[10] and compared with their major antagonists, actual or potential, they are ill-equipped and ill-supported. Their transport facilities reflect the inadequacies of the transport system of the whole country. At the same time of course the capabilities of the modern sector of the economy are reflected in the quite elaborate air-defence network which has been built up and the tremendous effort being put into developing nuclear weapons. This technological unevenness, however, will be very difficult to remedy; a nuclear and rocket programme *and* modernized army, navy and air forces would seem to be beyond the present capacity of Chinese industry.

The first task facing any Chinese force is to secure the frontiers of the country. This truism would be simpler if the frontiers could be easily defined but as has already been noted the modern Chinese state has had to struggle with exactly this problem: how to obtain general recognition of a territory called 'China'. China has no overseas bases and no overseas colonies but her geographical position is such that she has a long coast-line and a very long

[9] China is believed to have one G-class submarine with surface ballistic missile tubes but no operational missiles. More typically the navy contains vessels like the corvette built in Australia during the World War II ex-HMAS *Bendigo*, which was sold in Hong Kong for conversion into a merchant ship but found its way into the navy of the People's Republic where it was reconverted.

[10] Cf. Frank E. Armbruster, 'China's Conventional Military Capacity' in Tang Tsou (ed.), *op. cit.*

land boundary shared at present with no less than thirteen large or small non-Chinese territories. Except for the small areas of Hong Kong and Macao the contiguous territories are not settled with ethnic Chinese. The island dependencies of Taiwan, Quemoy and the Matsus do of course have Chinese populations but they present a major territorial problem of a different kind.

There is no question at all about the historical attitude of the Chinese to these particular territories. Taiwan has a few aboriginal people but has been settled for many centuries by Chinese from Fukien province. One of the generals who had supported the last Ming pretender in his struggles from the south against the Manchus finally retreated there and established an independent domain which lasted for twenty years before being absorbed by the Manchus in 1683. In 1895 a second alienation occurred when the island was seized by the Japanese and run as a successful Japanese colony for fifty years. It was restored to Chinese control in accordance with allied policy at the end of World War II. Traditionally-minded Chinese are fond of drawing historical parallels. In the seventeenth century the inheritors of the general who had established himself on Taiwan did not long enjoy their independence. A grandson finally saw the writing on the wall and swore allegiance to the new Manchu dynasty. If historical parallels were ever reliable the reincorporation of Taiwan might not be far off. In the meantime, however, the Communists take the Nationalist military threat with complete seriousness. They have consistently maintained a large number of combat-ready divisions in Fukien, opposite Taiwan.

Large numbers are also maintained in the industrial North-East where the border with Korea is a constant reminder of how quickly an invasion threat can arise. The border with the Soviet Union is very extensive. At both its Western and Eastern ends it represents the fruits of Tsarist expansion in the nineteenth century. In between lies the border with the People's Republic of Mongolia. Until recently these border areas had very few Chinese settlers but the Manchu dynasty had naturally been deeply concerned with their fate. The Manchus had expanded from their homeland in what we know as Manchuria to conquer first North and then South China and establish the Ch'ing dynasty. They had early come into conflict with Russian expansion in the seventeenth century and, after vigorous military action, signed the Treaty of Nerchinsk with the Russians in 1689. The boundary settlement in this treaty lacked precision but it certainly excluded the Russians from most of the Amur basin and left the Manchus in possession of all the Pacific coastal region for some 700 miles north of what is today Vladivostok.[11] In the era of Manchu decline, however, the Russians were able to obtain by 1860 vast stretches of territory north of the Amur River and, even more importantly, territory east of the Ussuri, which was to become known as the Maritime Province. Here at a fishing place known to the Chinese as Hai-shen-wei they established the port significantly named Vladivostok ('Lord of the East'). Russian interest in the area has not been confined to these places. Manchuria proper was occupied by Russia at the time of the Boxer rising and again in 1945–46 after the defeat of her imperial rival Japan in World War II. The Russian concession in Port Arthur was not finally abandoned until 1954. At the Western end China ceded extensive areas, by the Treaty of Ili (1881), which are now included in Soviet Kazakstan. Some areas here have remained in dispute and sections of the Soviet–Sinkiang border have never been delimited. The Soviet Government had talked about the need for 'redemarcation' in 1924 but has never shown any inclination to put into practice the celebrated Karakhan Declaration of 1919 in which Karakhan, the Deputy People's Commissar for Foreign Affairs had, on behalf of the infant Soviets, renounced all the concessions and territory obtained by the Tsarist treaties.

The border with Mongolia is the result of a Twentieth Century compromise whereby a buffer state has been created out of territory once under the control of the Ch'ing dynasty. There are undoubtedly nationalistically-minded Chinese who would like to see all the Mongol territory again under Chinese control. Mao himself told Edgar Snow in Yenan that this would be the proper solution and he apparently raised the subject when Khrushchev and Bulganin came to China in 1954. The Russians, however, refused to discuss the matter and insisted that the destiny of the Mongolian people must be determined in Ulan Bator and not in Peking or Moscow.[12] In practice Inner Mongolia has been absorbed as an

[11] See Alastair Lamb, *Asian Frontiers, op. cit.*, p. 205.
[12] See John Gittings, *Survey of the Sino-Soviet Dispute* (London: Oxford University Press for Royal Institute of International Affairs, 1968), pp. 166–67.

Autonomous Region of China and Outer Mongolia recognized as the People's Republic of Mongolia. Chen Yi told a press conference in September 1965 that refusal to recognize the People's Republic of Mongolia would be an example of 'Han [i.e. Chinese] chauvinism', an erroneous attitude in dealing with the minority peoples. The Inner Mongolian Autonomous Region of China has been heavily settled with Chinese (Han) settlers; the old outer region recognized, perhaps reluctantly, as in effect a Soviet protectorate.

With the consolidation of Chinese Communist control in both Manchuria and Sinkiang it is not surprising that the question of the validity of their borders should arise again. In 1963 China publicly declared that the treaties which established the present borders were 'unequal', typical of the settlements imposed on China by imperialist governments. The Soviet Government refused to accept this description and would not agree that such an admission should accompany a re-examination of the whole border. 'Naturally,' the Central Committee of the Communist Party of the Soviet Union argued in November 1963, 'we will not defend the Russian Tsars who permitted arbitrariness in laying down the state boundaries with neighbouring countries. We are convinced that you, too, do not intend to defend the Chinese emperors who by force of arms seized not a few territories belonging to others. But while condemning the reactionary actions of the top-strata exploiters who held power in Russia and in China at that time, we cannot disregard the fact that historically-formed boundaries between states now exist. Any attempt to ignore this can become the source of misunderstandings and conflicts.'[13]

Border incidents of differing degrees of seriousness have in fact been common in the past ten years. Some have been given much more publicity than others, depending on devious estimates by either party in the Sino–Soviet cold war of their propaganda value at different times. Both sides have charged the other with interference in the affairs of minority peoples on the Sinkiang–Soviet border. Disputes over fishing and navigation rights have been common on the river borders of Manchuria.

If the independence of Mongolia has had to be accepted as a fact no such attitude has been adopted towards Tibet. In Chinese eyes this is an outlying part of Chinese territory : when the Central

[13] Gittings, *op. cit.*, p. 162.

41

Government has been strong control of Tibet has been maintained; when it has been weak control has been lost. The Nationalists agree with Peking on this matter if on nothing else. They themselves, however, were never in a strong enough position to exercise effective control. As soon as the Communists were firmly enough established they reasserted their domination. No power in fact has ever recognized the existence of Tibet as a separate national state and China's allies during World War II generally agreed that China enjoyed some form of 'suzerainty' over Tibet, even though it was obvious that the Tibetans preferred a state of *de facto* independence.[14] (Tibetan appeals to the United Nations after the Chinese Communist invasion had little hope of getting very far. Apart from the difficulties of international law which made it hard to establish a clear case of aggression, the Chinese Nationalist representative on the Security Council differed from Peking on only one basic point : Tibet was part of the Republic of China, not part of the People's Republic.)

The question of the border with India was bound to arise as soon as Chinese control was effectively established in Tibet. The Indians soon noticed that many Chinese maps differed from some of their own in both the North-West and the North-East. They were later discomfited to find that without their knowledge the Chinese had built a road across the Aksai Chin area of the North West, linking Tibet with Sinkiang. Despite this evidence of lack of effective Indian control the Indian Government insisted on its claim. The Chinese argued that the whole dispute was a legacy of British Imperialism, that the boundary had never been formally delimited, let alone demarcated. The Tibetan uprisings in 1959 and the increased Chinese military activity involved in their suppression were accompanied by a number of border clashes. Attitudes hardened on both sides. Nehru's régime was denounced as controlled by the interests of India's big bourgeoisie and big landlords and clearly in league with the imperialists. It was accused of interfering in Tibet and coming under increasing United States influence, this country having taken over the British monopoly position. The actual Border War of 1962 had several curious features. Despite its obviously traumatic effect on the Indians, it does not appear to have been regarded as of great

14 See International Commission of Jurists, '*The Question of Tibet and the Rule of Law*' (Geneva, 1959), p. 91.

importance by the Chinese. At most three divisions moved into the North East Frontier Agency (NEFA). They inflicted a sharp defeat and then withdrew; they showed no inclination at all for a major campaign on the plains nor for the occupation of most of the territory in dispute. On the other hand they showed no inclination to withdraw in the North-West and have not done so. The military road from Tibet to Sinkiang remains in their hands and the preservation of their position there was probably their main objective. The NEFA action was something of a diversion.

Elsewhere they have not found it difficult to come to border agreements, with Burma, Pakistan, Bhutan and Nepal (despite a dispute as to who owns Mt Everest). The border with Laos and Vietnam has presented no problems. The variability of Peking's responses was strikingly illustrated during 1966 and 1967 in the two small imperialist enclaves of Macao and Hong Kong. In both places local activists inspired no doubt by the excitement of the Cultural Revolution thought that the time had come for a decisive blow against the imperialists. Peking clearly did not. In Macao the Portuguese authorities had to submit to a settlement with the Kwangtung Provincial authorities which clamped down on the activities of Chinese Nationalist sympathizers among other things, but did not basically alter the *modus vivendi* which had operated there for many years. Of the British colony the *People's Daily* observed sternly that 'Hong Kong has been Chinese territory since ancient times. This is a fact known to all, old and young in the world. More than a century ago British Imperialism came to China by pirate ships, provoked the criminal "opium war", massacred numerous Chinese people and occupied the Chinese territory of Hong Kong. Later it snapped the Chinese territory of Kowloon and the Chinese territory of the "New Territories". This is an enormous blood debt British imperialism owes to the Chinese people. Sooner or later the Chinese people will make a thoroughgoing liquidation of this debt with British imperialism.' This statement, (20 August 1967), not surprisingly took no notice of the different legal bases of British occupancy. The original British claim derives from the Treaty of Nanking when Hong Kong was taken as well as a large cash indemnity, as part of the settlement of the first Opium War. The Treaty of Peking, 1860, added the tip of the peninsula opposite, known as Kowloon. The much more extensive area of the New Territories, including the island of Lantau and many smaller islets were obtained on a ninety-nine year lease in 1898. This territory, an area of some 355 square miles, by far the largest part of the Crown Colony, is therefore held on a lease which has only another thirty years to run. Possibly 1997 will be considered a good year to make the thoroughgoing liquidation. Certainly 1967 was not thought to be it. The value of Hong Kong to the Chinese economy is still considered more important than an empty victory over British imperialism.

Even a brief survey reveals how difficult it is to discover something called Chinese Communist border policy. This is often discussed in terms of Chinese 'expansionism', as if China had some such innate tendency. (Do states ever suffer from 'contractionism'?) Chinese policy, however, appears to be more pragmatic than any general explanation would provide. China has been concerned to establish undisputed borders where she can, that is, where it is militarily, politically and economically practicable to do so. This has meant expanding in some places (Tibet) but not others (Mongolia), accepting Imperialists on the doorstep (Hong Kong, Macao) but not in force near industrial areas (Korea). It has meant accepting, with some reservation, the existing boundaries with the Soviet Union. It has meant a long drawn-out political struggle with the United States over Taiwan and the islands held by the Nationalists. Relations with the bordering states have been very variable. If it has ever been Peking's intention to have the small Communist states in Asia, North Korea, Mongolia, North Vietnam, as satellites it has certainly not succeeded in acquiring them. It has antagonized the most powerful, the Soviet Union, even if it has so far avoided a major military confrontation. It has conducted a punitive expedition against one, India, and cultivated excellent relations with another, Pakistan. It has increased its influence with the Himalayan kingdoms and lost it with Ulan Bator. Mongolia, after a period in which Chinese technical assistance was accepted has aligned itself firmly with the Soviet Union and reduced contact with China to a minimum. The Vietnam war, far from consolidating China's position as a leader of the Asian Communist states has been the occasion of many divisive arguments which have left China with little influence on the course of events. The great Communist debate over 'united action' in Vietnam and the refusal of China to co-operate with the Soviet

Union in forming a common Vietnam policy has only increased the bitterness of the Sino–Soviet dispute. The North Koreans have become more sympathetic to the Soviet arguments and the North Vietnamese less inclined than ever to listen to advice from Peking.

Despite its air of confidence the Chinese Communist régime has been troubled by a basic sense of insecurity. It came to power after many years fighting external and internal enemies but it was prevented from gaining complete victory when its opponents in the final civil war regained the active support of a great power, the United States. The outbreak of the Korean war so soon after the proclamation of the People's Republic was to have momentous consequences. China, it must be remembered, did not take part in the original attack by the North Koreans on the South. She intervened only when the North was in danger of defeat and MacArthur's forces were moving towards the Chinese border. Despite their initial successes the Chinese were in turn thrown back by the UN forces. Their losses were very heavy, they were clearly defeated in the air and the whole involvement was extremely expensive for them, militarily and politically.[15] The Soviet Union allowed them to bear great economic and military costs. The outcome of the war was barely satisfactory and its lessons are not likely to have been forgotten by the Chinese. The stalemate which resulted from the Korean truce and from the American protection of the Nationalists was not a reassuring one for the Chinese Communists. In a great arc around the Chinese coast the Americans consolidated their positions.

The development of American defence relations with South Korea, Japan and Taiwan, the establishment of SEATO and the increasing interest of the United States in South Vietnam and Thailand were all early indications to the Chinese of a shift in American global strategy throughout the 1950s. In the 1960s American strategy appeared to take an even more ominous turn as Asia increasingly displaced Europe as the centre of American concern. By 1966 American policy was regarded as set on a path of 'escalation' which was particularly dangerous for China. 'Because China holds aloft the banner of revolutions and extends unflinching support to revolutionary struggle everywhere, she is

[15] See the discussion of the war in Frank E. Armbruster, 'China's Conventional Military Capacity' in Tang Tsou, *op. cit.*, pp. 167–73.

looked upon by United States imperialism as the major obstacle to its schemes for world conquest, and therefore as its chief enemy –Washington's former Europe-first strategy has been upset and now abandoned because of the rising revolutionary movements in Asia and because of China's stand against United States imperialism.[16] The Americans were afraid of what they called 'a crisis of "falling dominoes" ' and were therefore engaged in a major redeployment of forces overseas which was designed to strengthen the military encirclement of China (See map on page 12).

According to the Chinese : 'Confrontation with China, instead of the Soviet Union, is the military strategy Washington now subscribes to. Thus, the Pentagon is trying to increase United States capability in conventional warfare instead of concentrating on fighting nuclear wars alone. Also, there is a shift to the development of conventional weapons which have been neglected over the past decades.'[17]

The hand of the imperialists could be seen in many places. Since the Quemoy crisis of 1958 it had been clear that the Soviet Union was not prepared to support China militarily in pursuit of a Chinese interest if this involved a risk of confrontation with the United States. Could the Soviets actually be in league with the Imperialists? This became the official thesis, a type of conspiracy theory which sees the hand of the bourgeoisie in the most unlikely places. In such a dangerous world one must be constantly on guard and tread carefully. Despite many brave words, Chinese policy has been to avoid pursuing any action which could lead to direct military confrontation with the more powerful imperialists. This does not mean that the struggle against them has been given up or that ultimate victory is not constantly proclaimed but that, since Korea, a low risk strategy has been consistently adopted, whenever the danger of imperialist intervention has been high.

[16] *Peking Review*, No. 7, 11 February 1966.
[17] *Peking Review*, No. 7, 11 February 1966.

Chapter Three

WAR AND POLITICS

As good Marxists and good Chinese, the Communist leaders have shown a great deal of interest in the lessons of history. As with other leaders, however, this has sometimes meant drawing bad analogies from the past to apply to the changed conditions of the present. Mao himself has always demonstrated a knowledge of the long history of China. His view of modern history has naturally been influenced by his own position in it and by the fact that the Chinese revolution, after a long struggle, succeeded under his leadership. As he believes that correct policy must follow from correct theory, it follows that his theories about how to conduct a revolutionary war are not only correct, but given their Marxist framework, universally applicable. His writings on the political and military aspects of the different stages of the revolution are extensive and are now sacrosanct. Lin Piao, his 'closest comrade in arms', has given them a convenient condensation in his celebrated article 'Long Live the Victory of People's War', written in 1965 ostensibly to celebrate the twentieth anniversary of the defeat of Japan in World War II. This was a victory, according to Lin, of the Chinese people led by the Communist Party of China and Chairman Mao over Japanese imperialism. It was part of the world struggle against fascism but that was particularly important because 'of the innumerable anti-imperialist wars waged by the Chinese people in the past hundred years, the war of resistance against Japan was the first to end in complete victory'[1].

The question Lin sets himself is how was it possible for a weak country like China to defeat a strong country like Japan? His answer makes no reference to the atomic bomb or indeed to the allied forces except to note that 'The Chinese people received support from the people and the anti-fascist forces all over the world.' The real basis of success was that the War of Resistance

[1] Lin Piao, 'Long Live the Victory of People's War'. Text for this and subsequent quotations in *Peking Review*, No. 36, 3 September 1965.

against Japan was 'a genuine people's war led by the Communist Party of China and Comrade Mao Tse-tung, a war in which the correct Marxist–Leninist political and military lines were put into effect.' The correct principles involved were first, a correct analysis of the principal contradictions in the situation and the different strengths of the opponents, leading to a realization that the war would be protracted and no quick victory could be realized. A protracted war must pass through three stages – strategic defence, strategic stalemate and finally strategic offensive. It means mobilizing, organizing and arming as many of the people as possible. The Party, that is to say, must follow United Front tactics: all who can be united against the enemy should be. As the peasantry provides the bulk of the population it must provide the bulk of the people's forces. The army will indeed be an army of a new type. A force of politicized peasants. It must have a new style of operations and a new style of work, sharply differentiated from the predatory armies of conscript peasants so much detested in the past. It will operate from rural base areas and will regard the capturing of cities as a task for the final stages of the war. Because of its initial weakness its primary style of warfare will be guerrilla fighting but it will pursue mobile warfare under suitable conditions. It will adhere to Mao's 'Basic Tactics' (not tackling superior forces head on, overstretching the enemy, getting him bogged down, eating a mouthful at a time and so on). At all times it will adhere to a policy of strong self-reliance.

The international significance of this general theory is spelled out analogically. 'Taking the entire globe, if North America and Western Europe can be called "the cities of the world", then Asia, Africa and Latin America constitute "the rural areas of the world". In a sense, the contemporary world revolution also presents a picture of the encirclement of cities by the rural areas. In the final analysis, the whole cause of world revolution hinges on the revolutionary struggles of the Asian, African and Latin American peoples. . . .' The Khrushchev revisionists of course have gone over to the enemy, are reluctant to acknowledge the strength of people's war, the primacy of man over weapons and the general correctness of Mao's theory. It will nevertheless triumph and United States imperialism and its lackeys will inevitably be defeated.

This article has provoked a flood of exegetical comment, much of it alarmist. It has been read by many as a blueprint for Chinese expansionism of a new type, a Chinese *Mein Kampf*, and it was not until the Cultural Revolution had run its course for some time that the *internal* significance of the article was more fully appreciated. It is a restatement of pure Maoist orthodoxy and as such was probably intended as an attack on unorthodox tendencies which were felt to be still strong in the country and especially in the armed forces. The struggle between two 'lines' on military affairs was not new. The Yenan-style revolutionary armies had obviously to face some changes when they became the regular forces of an established government but the contradiction between 'professionalization' and 'revolutionization' might have been hard to resolve.[2] The Cultural Revolution which was in full flood a year after Lin's article was published led to a great increase in the influence of the People's Liberation Army (PLA) in government but on the face of it it is an army very much under the control of old revolutionaries, not young professionals. The conflict of *red* and *expert* has been a constant theme in Chinese polemics and it will be necessary to return to this question again.

As an historical account of how the Japanese were defeated Lin's article is of course grossly deficient. It does not discuss the war in detail but simply asserts that the Chinese won because of their complete devotion to the thought of Mao Tse-tung. Few military men over the age of forty could be expected to swallow this whole, but the prudent ones knew how to act as if they did. The rate of turn-over of high staff officers in recent years is perhaps evidence that many of them have found it hard to keep up a show of complete Maoist orthodoxy. Elsewhere the boldness of the city–rural areas analogy might be expected to have a natural attraction for romantic revolutionaries. It seems hardly irrational to assert that revolutions will flourish in backward and under-developed countries. The notion that the 'Colonies and semi-colonies . . . represent the *world rural areas* in relation to the industrial countries which represent the world city' can be found, according to Clubb, as early as 1928 in the programme of the Communist International.[3] The idea that the revolution would

[2] See John Gittings, *The Role of the Chinese Army* (London: Oxford University Press for the Royal Institute of International Affairs, 1967).

[3] O. E. Clubb, *Twentieth Century China* (New York: Columbia University Press, 1964), p. 346.

flourish in the underdeveloped countries was later popular with the ill-fated Communist Party of Indonesia. The process by which such revolution, if successful, would undermine the highly developed world has not however been made clear. Such an expectation would seem to depend on a naïve view of the dependence of the developed economies on the undeveloped for raw materials which, if it ever was the case, no longer holds today. The developed countries, much to the cost of the undeveloped, can on the whole get along very nicely without worrying about the underdeveloped at all. The actual waging of People's War of course can be seen to have certain advantages if the developed countries (imperialists) can be drawn into protracted struggles abroad. Nothing unites like a common hate and alien troops can be guaranteed to generate dislike. A long-drawn-out struggle can be very costly in lives and money and can increase the tensions (contradictions) in the imperialist homeland.

Apart from this, would-be revolutionaries would do well to read carefully the list of conditions which Lin lays down for the successful prosecution of a People's War. Far from being a blueprint for the direct expansion of Chinese influence it argues that Revolution cannot be exported and that the people's forces must be almost entirely self-reliant. Despite its dogmatism it manages to be quite hard-headed about the conditions without which People's War cannot be expected to flourish. There is little of the mystique of Revolution here, no belief that Revolution can create its own conditions. A full-fledged People's War would have the following characteristics. First, the leadership of a strong Communist Party. Although the Party will use united front tactics and unite with whatever groups it can, it must not lose its identity or its leading role. Second, the army must accept the leading role of the Party and enjoy mass support, especially among the peasantry. Third, it must be possible to organize rural base areas, safe from enemy attack. Finally, even if a small amount of assistance is possible from fraternal socialist states, the People's forces must be essentially self-supporting and self-reliant. It does not take much imagination to see that this schematized picture of one stage of the Chinese revolution is not particularly easy to reproduce elsewhere. In many countries which might be thought to have a high potential for revolution one or more key conditions might still be absent. The local Communist Party might be full of revolutionary zeal but weak in organization. Many groups like religious organizations (which were of little importance to China) might be highly suspicious of united-front tactics; people who still trust their own institutions are often not prepared to accept a leading role for the local Communist Party. In many parts of the world, terrain of the kind which provided the Chinese with base areas does not exist and support from fraternal Parties is often very difficult to arrange. Where the peasantry is not predominantly 'poor' but by its own standards 'rich' and contented, revolutionary enthusiasm is not easily generated. Finally, where the opposing armed forces are aware of the problem facing them, guerrilla operations cannot be guaranteed to be successful.

In practice the Chinese have hailed every development in the world which might be thought to have revolutionary portent but their actual aid to revolutionary groups has been minimal. Even in Vietnam where Chinese aid has been important it is minuscule compared with the aid given by the Russians or by foreign governments to the anti-Communist régimes. The Chinese have on occasion been prepared to train people in Maoist doctrine and revolutionary techniques but they have not been prepared to commit their armed forces in support of such groups. Peking is often regarded as the conspirational centre of vast revolutionary plots. It could equally be regarded as a haven for not very successful revolutionary leaders as London was after 1848. A linguistic point is here worth noting. The Chinese term for 'revolution' (*Ko ming*) does not refer exclusively to the violent overthrow of governments any more than its English equivalent does. Any major change can be 'revolutionary'. A 'revolutionary upsurge' in the Chinese countryside for example does not imply that local government has been overthrown but rather that major social changes are said to be taking place in the countryside. When the Chinese say they are the centre of world revolution they are not saying that they are plotting the overthrow of all reactionary governments although they can always be expected to welcome such a 'change of fate'.

In an interview in September 1963 Chen Yi tried to explain the apparent contradictions in the doctrine to an Australian film director, John Dixon : 'The question of world revolution is one for the countries concerned. If countries are not ripe for revolution, then China can't do anything about it. However, China will support revolutions against imperialism and oppression. This is not to say that we are behind all revolutions. Castro in 1959 had no relationship with us, so therefore you can't blame China for the success of the Cuban revolution. China is not the arch-criminal behind every uprising. China cannot pour revolutions on or off when she wants to. China can only manage her own affairs. Revolutions depend on the people themselves. But China will support foreign revolutions both morally and politically. We are Marxists. We must support them. We don't care if we hurt the feelings of the United States, or even of Mr Khrushchev. We can't exchange this for our friendship with the oppressed people. But it must be noted, Chinese troops will not cross our borders to advance revolutions. China supports the efforts of all colonial, semi-colonial and oppressed peoples such as the American Negroes to liberate themselves. On the question of war we have to realize that wars are terrible things. Wars kill people. I've been a soldier for most of my life and seen a lot of fighting. If there is another war I can tell you now, that somebody else can do the fighting. I've seen enough. The United States has got to realize that we all live on the same globe. However, the colonial struggles will go on. Imperial policies disrupt the five principles of co-existence. The colonial struggles will go on and China stands with the oppressed. Peaceful co-existence – how can there be such a thing while there are oppressed? There can be Peaceful co-existence between sovereign states. This is China's policy. This does not include relations between oppressors and oppressed. The United States, and China have had many conflicts, but we've always been ready to settle our differences by peaceful negotiation. We initiated the Five Principles together with the Indians at Bandoeng and at Geneva. No one can cite an example of a violation of any of the five principles on China's part. Although we believe this, China will resist attack. You know, we were against the USSR shipping guided missiles to Cuba. We thought this was a very dangerous move which brought the world to the edge of war. Khrushchev is just an adventurer. China was not consulted on this move and we were entirely opposed to it. We didn't oppose the withdrawal of the missiles, but we did oppose the agreement which provided for the inspection of Cuba's sites. Disputes such as this should have been settled by peaceful negotiation. But none of this can alter the fact that there can be no Peaceful co-existence between oppressors and oppressed. And when the oppressed people of the world arise, don't blame us! We're not the ones who are acting aggressively. We have imperialist bases all around us. We don't have any bases in foreign countries, and we're not blockading anyone. For instance, Chinese air space is regularly violated by United States and Nationalist aircraft, and we have a war on our doorstep [Taiwan]. Yet when we protest, our Soviet friends blame us! – and not the Imperialists!'[4]

Maoist doctrine, in fact, is a curious mixture of revolutionary realism and revolutionary romanticism. It incites the oppressed to rise against their oppressors but it promises no Napoleonic crusades. In its own jargon it is resolutely opposed to 'Left' and to Right opportunism. It follows a correct 'line', naturally described as 'proletarian', which avoids any specific commitments. According to an article in the *Peking Review*, 'Within our Party and army, in recent decades and in all historical stages of the development of the Chinese revolution, there has always been a sharp and acute struggle between two diametrically opposed military lines. One is the proletarian military line represented by Chairman Mao, the other is the bourgeois military line advocated by opportunists of the 'Left' and Right. Chairman Mao's proletarian military line has been gradually developed and perfected in the course of this struggle against the bourgeois military line.'[5] The class tags need not distract us too much. They are necessary for a 'correct' formulation of the different lines but in themselves they tell us nothing. Behind them, nevertheless, it is possible to detect signs of real divergence of view on military doctrine. According to the article already quoted the main elements of Chairman Mao's military line are as follows :

1. In building the armed forces politics must be put first. The army is basically the military extension of the Party. 'Military affairs are only one means of accomplishing political tasks.' 'Military affairs must be subordinated to politics and politics must command military affairs.' The opposite line here is not so much military usurpation of the Party but what we would be inclined to call 'professionalism', putting 'technique' first, concentrating on

[4] Transcript of interview with John Dixon, 30 September 1963.
[5] 'Basic Differences Between the Proletarian and Bourgeois Military Lines', *Peking Review*, No. 48, 24 November 1967.

military theory and expertise, playing down political instruction and spending more time on purely military training.

2. The correct form of war is People's War which relies on mobilizing the masses. The opposing line is supposed to be the doctrine that 'weapons decided everything', that 'with new technical equipment any invading enemy can be annihilated on the sea, in the air or at the base from which it launches its attack'. It is not clear whether this is to imply a doctrine of reliance on nuclear weapons, but it is supposed to imply a denial of the need for large militia forces, for arming the masses. On the contrary, 'Our great leader Chairman Mao has fully and most profoundly explained the importance of arming the masses. After country-wide victory, Chairman Mao told us time and again : "The imperialists are bullying us in such a way that we will have to deal with them seriously. Not only must we have a powerful regular army, we must also organize contingents of the people's militia on a big scale. This will make it difficult for the imperialists to move a single inch in our country in the event of invasion. Should the imperialists dare to unleash an aggressive war against our country, then we will turn the whole nation into soldiers; the militia will co-operate with the People's Liberation Army and at any time replenish it to crush the aggressors utterly." '

3. Chairman's Mao's 'consistent strategic concept' is said to be the notion of 'active defence'. Again in the case of an invasion of China this would involve not the taking up of defensive positions but a policy of luring the enemy in deeply, concentrating superior forces and fighting decisive battles of annihilation when the circumstances were favourable. Finally:

4. 'Weapons are an important factor in war, but not the decisive factor; it is people, not things, that are decisive. Final victory or defeat in war is determined by the ground forces in fighting successive battles, by the political consciousness and courage of the people and their spirit of sacrifice, by fighting with rifles, hand-grenades and bayonets, by hand-to-hand engagements, night-fighting and fighting over a range of tens of metres. In combating an imperialist war of aggression, no matter what weapons the enemy may use, if they dare to go deep into our country, we will enjoy the maximum initiative, give full play to our strong points and advantages, use various methods to deal them blows, vigorously demonstrate the magic power of people's

war and make sure that the aggressors will never go back alive.'
'They', the opposition liners, are supposed to have clamoured
that now 'conditions are different'. The answer to this is definitive : 'What conditions are different? The imperialists do indeed
have atomic bombs and nuclear weapons. But this is not so
terrific! Marxists have at all times held that no matter what
changes take place in technical equipment that basic laws of
revolutionary war will never change.'[6] Marx himself might have
been rather startled by the latest assertion.

In this kind of argument it is natural for Europeans to look for
evidence of clashes between politicians and generals, Party men
and military men but these antitheses are very misleading in the
Chinese setting. Although the Party was created, like most revolutionary parties, by intellectuals it was forced to become highly
militarized. It finally came to power not by revolutionary coup
but as a result of over twenty years of war. Its leaders have nearly
all had extensive military experience in the Red Armies which
were simply the military expression of the Party. The established
armed forces of the People's Republic – the People's Liberation
Army (PLA) – have continued to be officered by Party men. The
idea of the military as a special professional group is anathema to
Mao. The idea that military matters and military men should be
kept clear of politics would strike him as both absurd and dangerous. Military affairs and political affairs are inseparable; military
doctrine cannot be separated from political doctrine. They can
of course be analytically distinguished but such analysis should
only be used to demonstrate the primacy of politics.

It is not surprising therefore that the role of the PLA has
hardly been comparable to the role of professional armies in
Europe or in the Soviet Union. In recent years it has acted as a
source of agricultural labour, a training school for new cadres
and as patron of the arts. Its soldiers have been held up as models
of moral perfection, of selfless devotion to the people and Chairman Mao, as model students of his thought. It has therefore had
a major role in education and propaganda. In the turbulence of
the Cultural Revolution it has been politically involved in the
most direct way even though in the early stages it appeared to
stand aloof. The construction of a new type of provincial administration with direct participation by the People's Liberation

[6] *Peking Review*, No. 48, 24 November 1967, same article.

Army has enhanced its political role. The PLA in short is supposed to embody most perfectly the thought of Chairman Mao. 'In the great proletarian cultural revolution, the PLA has undertaken the glorious but arduous tasks of supporting the Left, assisting industry and agriculture, exercising military control and giving military and political training. The commanders and fighters of the PLA are boundlessly loyal to our great leader and supreme commander Chairman Mao and to the great thought of Mao Tse-tung. They do what Chairman Mao says, displaying the noble quality of the PLA.'[7]

A significant number of leaders of the PLA have found it difficult, however, to keep their political balance and their positions during the Cultural Revolution. The grounds for the dismissal of many of them are far from clear but some of the policy issues which have been in dispute can be discerned in the renewed attacks on Peng Teh-huai who was dismissed as Minister of Defence as long ago as 1959. Peng may or may not have been guilty of some of the things he has been charged with but it seems certain that he did attack the Commune programme. In the words of one attack on him 'He slandered as an "exaggerated trend" the vigorous campaign launched by hundreds of millions of people to build socialism under the guidance of Mao Tse-tung's thought, claiming that "the gains could not compensate for the losses". He flung mud at the people's communes, saying that they were "set up too early" and were "a mess". He vilified as "petty-bourgeois fanaticism" the mass movement and the revolutionary drive and zeal of the people, and viciously attacked our great leader Chairman Mao. At and after the 20th Congress of the Communist Party of the Soviet Union, Khrushchev stirred up an adverse current to oppose the so-called "personality cult" of Stalin. Trailing close behind him, Peng Teh-huai strove to impair Chairman Mao's immensely high prestige.' This probably goes to the heart of the matter but it seems unlikely that, as the indictment claims, he had consistently plotted against Mao for thirty years! The charges against him are of interest, however, as an indication of elements of the 'bourgeois military line', that is, policies opposed to Chairman Mao's. According to the article just cited, 'Peng Teh-huai directed his spearhead first of all against the great thought of Mao Tse-tung. In a malicious attack, he

[7] *Peking Review*, No. 36, 1 September 1967.

56

alleged : "Mao Tse-tung's military thinking is now out-of-date and no longer applicable". In the training programmes he mapped out for the army and military academies, the study of Chairman Mao's works was never incorporated as the fundamental principle and major content. Using the pretext of modernizing the army and putting it on a regular basis, Peng Teh-huai desperately opposed giving prominence to proletarian politics. He gave first place to military technique and denied that political and ideological work is the primary factor in building up an army's combat strength. He tried to abolish political work in the army, the democratic system and the mass line and undermine the principle of unity between officers and men and between superiors and subordinates. Chairman Mao has consistently upheld the principle of People's War : victory in a revolutionary war is achieved through relying on the masses, arming them and turning all the people into soldiers. After nation-wide victory, in order to consolidate the dictatorship of the proletariat and guard against imperialist aggression, the significance of People's War greatly increased rather than diminished. But under the pretext that the situation had changed and the militia system was now "out-of-date", Peng Teh-huai tried to abolish the nation-wide militia system and totally negate the principle of People's War. His wrong ideas on the question of militia building were a continuation and development of his long-standing warlord mentality and purely military viewpoint which rejected People's War and reliance on the masses. Peng Teh-huai opposed the strategic principle of active defence formulated by Chairman Mao. He adopted a completely passive attitude towards preparations for dealing with United States imperialist aggression. He did not proceed from the standpoint of preparedness against war. Instead, he adopted the opportunist attitude that "no fighting would break out and that war was unlikely". In a futile attempt to turn our army into an appendage of the Khrushchev revisionist clique, he depended entirely on that clique for the improvement of our army's equipment and the development of up-to-date military science and technology. He totally disregarded the needs of the proletarian revolutionary cause and the safety of the motherland.'[8]

[8] 'Settle Accounts with Peng Teh-huai for His Heinous Crimes of Usurping Army Leadership and Opposing the Party', *Peking Review*, No. 36, 1 September 1967.

THE SECURITY OF CHINA

The problem of modernization of the Chinese forces has not been simply a technical one. Mao has suspected, and rightly, that a great deal more has been involved than the provision of up-to-date equipment and modern technical training. The growth of professional attitudes, procedural routine and military bureaucracy have naturally contrasted sharply with the Yenan spirit of revolutionary fervour, improvization and rough democracy. The Red Armies were supposed to be without rank but ranks were introduced in the PLA under Peng Teh-huai in 1955 when a great flurry of uniforms appeared and the silk factories began turning out embroidered pictures of marshals complete with elaborate caps and decorations. Ten years later under Lin Piao rank was abolished again and everyone reappeared in the same basic uniform. How an army functions without rank has always been a puzzle to outsiders. A hierarchy does of course exist but in theory, apparently, no one has substantive rank; appointment to a particular command post carries a certain rank which is relinquished on leaving it. This is supposed to illustrate military democracy but without detailed knowledge of how postings are made and transfers arranged it is difficult to estimate whether the system produces more democracy or simply a higher level of arbitrariness. Mao has consistently distrusted bureaucratism and professionalism. There has always been something of the inspired amateur about him. It is highly characteristic of him that, in the early Commune directives which are very much in his style, the very idea of functional specialization should be attacked. In the new society everyone would at the same time be a farmer, a worker, a trader, a student and a soldier; the age-old distinctions between mental and manual worker, townsman and countryman would disappear. Militarily this was supposed to mean that every able-bodied adult in China would be in a militia unit!

It is not really surprising that military professionals should have quietly sabotaged this grandiose project. The task of organizing and training, let alone arming, several hundred million peasants in militia units would daunt even the PLA. The modern history of the militia in China provides a good example of the gap which often exists between ideological aspiration and practical reality. From Gittings's account it is clear that there has often been a lack of enthusiasm for the idea of the militia as a mass military movement.[9] In the anti-Japanese war the militia forces were an important supplement to the Red Army units. They formed the élite of the Self-Defence units operating behind the Japanese lines and provided a basis for the great expansion of the Communist armies in 1945. By 1950 there were said to be some five and a half million men in the militia, and a programme of expansion began after the outbreak of the Korean war. The target for expansion, however, 23,750,000 or some 5 per cent of the population, was apparently not reached.

Militia men continued to maintain local security but not until 1957 were they integrated with the reserve system of the army. When the 'Everyone a Soldier' movement was launched in 1958 it was announced as an innovation of great importance, 'a new development of Comrade Mao Tse-tung's strategic thinking on the People's War'. Within four months all eligible people were supposed to have responded to the Chairman's call and enrolled in the militia. In January 1969 it was said to total no less than 220 million men and women. Only a small proportion of them, however, seem to have been systematically trained. In places where the militia was efficiently organized its activities often interfered with agricultural production. In the bad years of 1959 and 1960 its organization deteriorated to such an extent that the Military Affairs Committee of the Central Committee ordered a complete overhaul. In some areas the militia had simply disintegrated, in others 'bad elements' had used it to oppress the local populace. Control over the militia's access to arms was tightened, emphasis was put on increasing production and militia units were placed under firm PLA control. Since 1962 the doctrine of 'Everyone a Soldier' has continued to be part of Maoist orthodoxy but training in the militia has in fact been confined to a minority.

It is also not surprising that some PLA leaders should have doubted the wisdom of the break with the Soviet Union. In the first years after 1949 when the Sino–Soviet alliance was declared absolutely unshakeable and indissoluble the PLA leant very heavily on the Soviet Union for re-equipment. The air force was created almost entirely with Soviet equipment. The Chairman might preach self-reliance but military-industrial self-reliance cannot in fact be created overnight, no matter how much

[9] See Gittings, *The Role of the Chinese Army, op. cit.*, Chapter X.

voluntaristic rhetoric is invoked. It is equally not surprising that there should have been disagreements about the likelihood of war with the imperialists breaking out. On this point Mao himself may well have changed his mind more than once. After the escalation of the Vietnam war in 1965 there appears to have been mounting apprehension in China that the United States might extend the war to China. The irrepressible Chen Yi said in October 1965 that he had gone grey waiting for the imperialists to attack.[10] In September 1966, however, he told a delegation of Japanese parliamentarians that he did not believe the United States would invade China and that he did not take a particularly pessimistic view of relations with the United States.[11] There is no great inconsistency in Chinese eyes in these sorts of statements. The imperialists can never be trusted but it might on occasion be possible to reach accommodation with them. There was always the possibility nevertheless that the more irrational elements among them might unleash a war.

It is on the question of how to deal with this contingency that Mao seems to have been most inflexible. His defence doctrine appears to provide very little comfort to the professionalizers in the PLA. It is assumed that an imperialist attack on China will have to be met by China herself. The Soviet Union will not be of any assistance. The imperialists might well use long-range nuclear-strikes in combination with bacteriological and chemical warfare. With a country the size of China, however, these measures would not be enough to achieve victory. Such attacks would have to be followed up by invasion by ground forces if the defeat of China was to be achieved. Such attacks, however, would be countered by People's War, 'a protracted, broken-back war supported by "aroused masses" of people and fought by the large regular forces, local forces, and a massive militia developed under the concept "everyone a soldier". These forces would combine mobile conventional war with widespread, independent guerrilla warfare.'[12] 'The doctrine calls not only for a strategy of active defence in depth, but also for a policy of trading space for time. The Chinese

[10] Press Conference. Text in *Peking Review*, No. 41, 8 October 1965.

[11] Donald S. Zagoria, *Vietnam Triangle* (New York: Pegasus, 1967), p. 97.

[12] Ralph L. Powell, 'Maoist Military Doctrine', *Asian Survey*, April 1968.

forces must "dare to lure the enemy in deep". Hostile forces will be "bogged down in endless battles" and "drowned in a hostile human sea".[13] In the end the invading forces will be worn down, defeated piecemeal and finally driven from the country. As Chou En-lai stated in May 1966 : 'China is prepared. Should the United States impose a war on China, it can be said with certainty that, once in China, the United States will not be able to pull out, however many men it may send over and whatever weapons it may use, nuclear weapons included. Since the 14 million people of southern Vietnam can cope with over 200,000 United States troops, the 650 million people of China can undoubtedly cope with 10 million of them. No matter how many United States aggressor troops may come, they will certainly be annihilated in China.

'Once the war breaks out, it will have no boundaries. Some United States strategists want to bombard China by relying on their air and naval superiority and avoid a ground war. This is wishful thinking. Once the war gets started with air or sea action, it will not be for the United States alone to decide how the war will continue. If you can come from the sky, why can't we fight back on the ground? That is why we say the war will have no boundaries once it breaks out.'[14]

The whole doctrine, as Powell points out depends 'on the doubtful assumption that after initial long-range nuclear strikes, the United States would invade China with land forces'. The plan is both a supreme example of orthodox-Maoist military thinking and also a doctrine of necessity. Without a credible nuclear deterrent 'Maoist leaders still have no alternative but to develop the best possible conventional and revolutionary defence against a possible nuclear attack, or depend on a Soviet nuclear umbrella, which they are unwilling to do. The leadership hopes that the announced determination to fight a protracted "People's War" will serve as a deterrent by convincing their enemies that an attempt to conquer China would be too costly'.[15] The whole defence doctrine, however, has attracted much less attention in the West than the possible development of a nuclear deterrent, an answer to the imperialists in their own terms.

[13] Powell, op. cit., p. 243.
[14] Statement in Peking Review, No. 20, 13 May 1966.
[15] Powell, op. cit., p. 245.

Chapter Four

NUCLEAR WEAPONS

One of Mao's most celebrated images – the paper tiger – has been misunderstood almost as often as it has been derided. To say that imperialism is a paper tiger is not to say that it is powerless; it is to say in a hyperbolic fashion that it is not as powerful as it looks. The image was invoked by Mao in a conversation in 1946 with the indomitable Anna Louise Strong, a figure revered in Peking, where she has lived for many years as the recipient of 'a very important statement'. In his 'Talk With The American Correspondent Anna Louise Strong' Mao discusses the possibility of the United States launching a war against the Soviet Union:

'*Strong:* Suppose the United States uses the atom bomb? Suppose the United States bombs the Soviet Union from its bases in Iceland, Okinawa and China?

'*Mao:* The atom bomb is a paper tiger which the United States reactionaries use to scare people. It looks terrible, but in fact it isn't. Of course, the atom bomb is a weapon of mass slaughter, but the outcome of a war is decided by the people, not by one or two types of weapons.

'All reactionaries are paper tigers. In appearance, the reactionaries are terrifying, but in reality they are not so powerful. From the long term point of view, it is not the reactionaries but the people who are really powerful. In Russia, before the February Revolution in 1917, which side was really strong? On the surface the Tsar was strong but was swept away by a single gust of wind in the February Revolution. In the final analysis the strength in Russia was on the side of the Soviets of Workers, Peasants and Soldiers. The Tsar was just a paper tiger. Wasn't Hitler once considered very strong? But history proved that he was a paper tiger. So was Mussolini, so was Japanese imperialism. On the contrary, the strength of the Soviet Union and of the people in all countries who loved democracy and freedom proved much greater than had been foreseen.

China too, is a big country, but one day we're going to catch up with them in strength.

'It's the same with the USSR – they do not treat with us on a basis of equality. They think that they are an orchestra conductor and that we must alway follow their baton. They act as if we must always listen to their orders. But this is their leadership. The Russian people are good, and their social system is good. Khrushchev in his policy towards China is quite wrong. China insists that any negotiations must be conducted on the basis of equality! The heavens will not fall down if we disagree with them. They can do as they please, but we will build our own strength up. The China question will only be solved by China standing up for herself.'

He went on to philosophize about China's situation and her need to become strong and self-reliant. 'We don't believe in the doctrine of the other cheek. China requires a hundred years to become a modern state. We have made, and we will make many mistakes, because we lack experience. As I say, it will take a hundred years. In the past we thought we could do it in ten. But that was wrong. However, our direction is right and our country is united. You know, external hostility can be a good thing. It makes us stand up together. No one can give us protection, in fact, because they always attach conditions and they want to control us. In a way, we must thank those who blockade us, because we can then turn round to our people and say – "If you don't work and produce more, if you don't study and learn more, those outsiders will move in and control us". This is one of the greatest stimuli China has. Otherwise we might relax and get soft.

'On the other hand, we are willing to have more contacts with other nations. We don't feel isolated. We are willing to trade more. We have diplomatic relations with forty different countries and we don't want to break off the Warsaw talks. But the United States must take the first step. Must make a gesture, otherwise nohing will result.'

Nuclear weapons are the supreme symbol of national self-reliance. Although the Chinese have not spelt out their nuclear doctrine in any great detail they have revealed enough of their motivation to make comparison possible with the French case. B. W. Augenstein has been able to collate numbers of statements which reveal a high degree of similarity in the Chinese and French positions. Both see the development of national nuclear forces as 'the marks of national greatness, and political power and importance'.[6] The Chinese would probably agree with the French arguments that 'the science and technology required for a modern weapons programme contribute to the general economy, rather than draining it'; that it may even 'produce direct benefits by reducing overall military expenditure'.[7] They would probably also agree that states without nuclear weapons tend to be ignored by those which have them. Both are sceptical about relying on the nuclear power of allies.

China has never been the centre of a military alliance-system, and her one major military alliance, established in the Sino–Soviet Treaty of Friendship, Alliance and Mutual Assistance, February 1950 has hardly been an encouraging example to follow. The Soviet Union had previously concluded a treaty with the Republic of China in 1945. This had provided for mutual military aid in the event of any future attack by Japan on either party. The 1950 Treaty provided that the parties would 'undertake jointly to take all the necessary measures at their disposal for the purpose of preventing a repetition of aggression and violation of peace on the part of Japan or any other State which should unite with Japan, directly or indirectly, in acts of aggression. In the event of one of the High Contracting Parties being attacked by Japan or States allied with it, and thus being involved in a state of war, the other High Contracting Party will immediately render military and other assistance with all the means at its disposal.'

Soviet spokesmen have claimed that the Treaty has had a major deterrent effect and protected China from attack by the United States during the Korean war, and during the off-shore islands crisis of 1958. There may be some justification for the former claim; uncertainty about Soviet reactions probably did help to dissuade President Truman from accepting the advice of those who wanted to extend the war into China. In the latter case Khrushchev's statement of support for China came only after the crisis had passed its peak and China had proposed that ambassadorial talks between China and the United States be resumed. It did little to increase China's confidence in Soviet support in the event of a Sino–American war. According to Article VI, the 1950

[6] B. W. Augenstein, 'The Chinese and French Programs for the Development of National Nuclear Forces', *Orbis*, XI, No. 3, 1967.

[7] Augenstein, *op. cit.*, p. 853.

Treaty will be valid for thirty years with the option at the end of this term of renewals for five-yearly periods. With the worsening of Sino–Soviet relations, however, increasing doubts have been cast by both sides on the value of the Treaty. In 1963 Chen Yi, as already noted, declared Soviet promises of support to be worthless. On the fifteenth anniversary of the Treaty, in February 1965, he expanded on the 'militant friendship' of the Chinese people for the Soviet people which was embodied in the Treaty but was noticeably lukewarm about the Soviet Government. The anniversary does not appear to have been observed since 1966. By 1967 Chinese papers were openly calling for the overthrow of the 'New Tsars in the Kremlin'. By 1969 they were reporting with indignation the contacts being made by the Soviet Government with the Chinese Nationalists.[8]

The successful bomb tests have been hailed in official communiqués as 'a great inspiration and support' to all peoples in their revolutionary struggles, but no circumstances have been described or even hinted at in which China would contemplate using her nuclear weapons on behalf of any ally or any revolutionary group. On 20 September 1968 Zeri i Popullit, the Albanian Party paper, implied in an editorial that in the event of an attack on Albania China would come to her assistance possibly with nuclear backing. But no such undertaking has been admitted by China and there are indications that none is intended.[9]

China has professed herself equally opposed to both nuclear 'overlords', the United States and the Soviet Union. 'The Soviet revisionist ruling clique often brandishes its nuclear weapons, boasting about its "protection" of mankind and pretending to be its "saviour". But people have seen how Khrushchev's bluff failed in the Caribbean crisis. Later, Khrushchev and his successors, Brezhnev and Kosygin, threw off all disguises and openly con-

[8] See, for example, 'Soviet Revisionists Step Up Counter-Revolutionary Collusion With Chiang Kai-shek Bandit Gang', Peking Review, No. 11, 14 March 1969, which referred to the visit of 'a Soviet citizen going by the name of Victor Louis' to Taiwan and the unofficial contacts of Nationalist and Soviet diplomats. 'These facts show to what depths the Soviet revisionist renegade clique, collaborating with US imperialism, has sunk in its criminal collusion with the Chiang gang in viciously opposing the great People's Republic of China.'
[9] See the account by John Gittings in the Far Eastern Economic Review, 29 September 1968.

cluded one dirty nuclear deal after another with United States imperialism. Washington not only feels perfectly at ease with nuclear weapons being in the hands of the Soviet revisionist clique, but also plots with the Kremlin to oppose socialist China. Facts have proved to the hilt that the nuclear weapons in the hands of the Soviet revisionist clique, like those in the hands of the United States imperialists, are for the purpose of intimidating the revolutionary people of the whole world, and for opposing the revolution and the people.'[10] This was the response of the *People's Daily* to the speech in which Secretary McNamara announced the decision to build an anti-ballistic-missile system specifically directed against China. Chinese attitudes to the Test Ban Treaty, and the Non-Proliferation Treaty have been similar: both are merely examples of collusion between the great powers to prevent the erosion of their dominant position in the world.

'On the question of nuclear weapons, the United States and the Soviet Union have long stood together in jointly opposing China and the revolutionary people of the world; their policy is "nuclear colonialism" pure and simple. The Soviet revisionist clique's fig-leaf of anti-imperialist pretensions has been torn aside in the course of the development of international class struggle, and by now practically nothing is left.'[11] The idea of 'nuclear protection' being given to the non-nuclear subscribers to the Treaty was naturally denounced as simply a device to establish 'protectorates'. 'It must be pointed out that this nuclear fraud of United States imperialism and Soviet revisionism is also a component part of their anti-China plot. They not only want to fan up anti-China feelings internationally through the so-called "treaty on non-proliferation of nuclear weapons" but also want to accelerate the rigging up of an anti-China encirclement by providing their "nuclear umbrella" to India and other countries bordering China. The United States imperialists and the Soviet revisionists have thus taken a big step forward in their military collaboration against China. [They] are incorrigible devotees of nuclear fetishism. They believe that with a scrap of paper such as the "treaty on non-proliferation of nuclear weapons" they will be able to preserve their nuclear monopoly and, on the strength of the nuclear

[10] Text in *Peking Review*, No. 44, 27 October 1967.

[11] *People's Daily*, 8 July, 1968. Text in *Peking Review*, No. 28, 12 July 1968.

weapons in their hands, to hold back the tide of the revolution of the world's people. This is day-dreaming pure and simple ! The nuclear monopoly held by the United States imperialists and Soviet revisionists was broken long ago and will certainly be broken again.'[12]

Apart from this type of rhetoric which certainly shows something of the psychology of the Chinese leadership, very little has been published in China which could be regarded as indicative of future nuclear strategy. China is not yet a major nuclear power despite the successful explosion of a number of bombs. Very little information has been released by China about the development of nuclear technology or the progress of the missile programme. From analysis by foreign scientists of the fall-out resulting from the bombs a certain amount of hard information has been obtained. It is also known that a guided missile has been successfully tested. These facts have been enough to cause a flood of speculation about Chinese intentions and the scale, direction and timing of the Chinese nuclear and missile programmes. These estimates have been rather variable and tend to reflect the assumptions of different intelligence agencies about what is likely rather than detailed knowledge. A certain amount of see-sawing in the estimates is detectable. Most observers originally were sceptical of China's ability to develop an atomic bomb without substantial outside assistance. It was only in 1958 that Chinese spokesmen revealed the intention to develop nuclear weapons.[13] The first atomic bomb test was nevertheless achieved by 1964, the first hydrogen bomb test by 1967. The atomic bombs did not use

[12] *People's Daily*, 13 June 1958. Text in *Peking Review*, No. 25, 21 June 1968.

[13] Chü Hao-jan has pointed out a linguistic curiosity in the original version of what Mao himself said on the subject in June 1958. The sentence frequently quoted in press translations reads 'Our great leader Chairman Mao pointed out as far back as June 1958: I think it is entirely possible for some atom bombs and hydrogen bombs to be made in ten years' time'. The original phrase, *i tiar yüan tzu tan* (used for example in the *People's Daily* of 18 June 1967) has been translated as 'some atomic bombs' but it could be more colloquially rendered as 'a bit of an atomic bomb'. The phrase perhaps reveals the ambivalence in Mao's own attitude to nuclear weapons; on the one hand he is well aware of the great military and political prestige attached to them; on the other hand his views on the primacy of man over weapons leads him to regard technological innovation as comparatively unimportant.

plutonium as had been expected but Uranium 235. The separation of this from the U 238 isotope is not easy and implies the development of a highly specialized technology.

Once it became clear that China was engaged in missile research a counter tendency appeared in many estimates – in trying to avoid underestimating Chinese capabilities analysts have tended to minimize the difficulties facing any Chinese missile programme. There is no doubt that China has physicists and engineers of world repute who are capable of directing advanced missile research. Chien Hsueh-sen, for example, who is a key figure in the research programme was recognized as a leading expert in the United States before his return to China. The Scientific and Technological Commission for National Defence has had a military chairman since its formation in 1958 and the Military Commission of the Central Committee of the Party has probably had high-level control over the nuclear and missile programme. It has been generally believed that this military control helped to insulate the scientific and technical workers from the more extreme political upsets of recent years and there was some justification for this view before 1967. For instance, the resolution of the Central Committee of 8 August 1966 which endorsed the programme of the Great Proletarian Cultural Revolution specifically ruled that 'As regards scientists, technologists, and ordinary members of working staffs, as long as they are patriotic, work energetically, and are not against the party and socialism, and maintain no illicit relations with any foreign country, we should in the present moment continue to apply the policy "unity, criticism, unity". Special care should be taken of those scientists and technical personnel who have made contributions. Efforts should be made to help them gradually transform their world outlook and style of work.'

This, however, did not prevent the outbreak of faction fighting in some branches of the Chinese Academy of Sciences and the formation of a new controlling committee for that body. In 1967 and 1968 many reports were published of attacks on leading scientists for relying too heavily on foreign methods and foreign textbooks and maintaining contacts with revisionist scientists abroad. Special conferences of scientists and technologists went through the ritual of denouncing revisionist leadership in defence science. Some 'revolutionary' groups attacked figures as important as Nieh

Jung-chen, the head of the Scientific and Technological Commission for National Defence but he, like other high-ranking Party men, survived the attacks. It is impossible to determine how far such disruptions have interfered with research and development but it is obvious that the military authorities have exercised some restraints even though the military politicians, led by Lin Piao, have been deeply involved in the politics of the Cultural Revolution. The whole nuclear and missile programme which has been under their direction is now claimed as a special triumph for the Thought of Mao Tse-tung and a special triumph over the revisionist influence of Liu Shoo-chi.

Even if the scientists and technologists have been comparatively insulated from the immediate effects of the Cultural Revolution there is little doubt that its longer-term effects on research will be severe. All schools and universities closed down in July 1966 pending sweeping changes in selection and admission procedures, and the total reconstruction of curricula. Many were still closed more than twelve months later and the restructuring of the educational system is still proceeding. The competition to gain admittance to the best schools and universities had been extremely fierce and undoubtedly many children with bourgeois backgrounds had had scholastic advantages in the competitive examination system. Under the new system social origin and 'redness' will presumably be even more important than before in determining career lines. The old education system has been attacked as élitist, dominated by bourgeois values, expensive and long-drawn out. In the Maoist era the educational course will be shorter and less theoretical; book learning will be minimized and students encouraged to solve practical problems and work at production.

It cannot be denied that Chinese education in the past tended to be formalistic, deferential to authorities, bookish and repetitive. Whether a demoralized teaching profession will be able to revolutionize the system in a few years remains to be seen. Certainly in the short run there has been considerable disruption and the flow of highly trained manpower must have been interrupted. The long-term effects on the production of first-class research scientists and engineers cannot be calculated.

China is still living on scientific capital in the form of many highly qualified men who received their higher education abroad but returned to China. Most of them work in research institutes where facilities are impressive. They are well supplied with foreign journals and literature but the opportunities for stimulating contacts with foreign scientists are rare and the opportunities for further training abroad rarer still.[14]

Very little attention appears to have been given to the problems of connecting the research work done in specialized institutes with the teaching required in universities; outside their institutes scientists seem to have few teaching responsibilities. The need for higher research and teaching to go hand in hand is a cliché which should appeal to Maoists but it does not appear to have been generally recognized in China. In short, it will not be surprising if a lack of highly skilled manpower is one of the fruits of the Maoist era.

Even if the skilled manpower is available China must face formidable developmental problems in the nuclear field. A small stockpile of atomic bombs does not make China a major nuclear power. For a minimum deterrent effect some means of delivery must exist. The only bombers available to China are old, slow and of limited range. They would be unable to penetrate any modern air defence. As China has made no effort to replace these aircraft it has been assumed that she has opted for a missile-delivery system. A guided missile has certainly been launched, possibly with a range of some 500 miles, but the range is not known for certain, nor is the capacity of the warhead. (The Chinese announcement of 27 October 1966, said only that the missile 'accurately hit the target at the appropriate distance, effecting a nuclear explosion'.) The development of medium-range missiles, capable of travelling 1,500 miles has been estimated as likely by 1969, with missiles of 2,000 to 4,000 miles range feasible by 1970 and inter-continental ballistic missiles with a range of 5,000 to 10,000 miles possible by the mid-1970s. The technical problems involved in developing suitable warheads and guidance mechanisms are not beyond China's capabilities but the necessary production-engineering is both complex and expensive. Any full-

[14] The Cultural Revolution has led to the cancellation of almost all student exchange, the departure of foreign students from China and the return of Chinese students abroad. See Stewart E. Fraser, 'China's International, Cultural and Educational Relations', *Comparative Education Review*, Vol. XIII, No. 1, February 1969. Compare, also, John M. H. Lindbeck, 'An Isolationist Science Policy', *Bulletin of the Atomic Scientists*, February 1969.

scale development of missiles will raise further problems in testing. For ranges up to 2,000 miles tests can presumably be carried out in Sinkiang but for inter-continental missiles the only obvious area is the Pacific Ocean. To conduct successful tests into the Pacific the navy would have to be considerably expanded to manage the tracking and recovery of the missiles. So far there does not appear to be any evidence of such a naval programme.

Whether China will in fact follow the lines of missile development which have been mapped out for her by interested observers will not be known until evidence of a series of tests, as contrasted with isolated tests of devices with different properties, is available. It is not at all obvious what, in Chinese eyes, would constitute a credible nuclear deterrent, that is a force sufficient to deter an attack by either of the super-powers, the United States or the Soviet Union, or by one of their allies. The nuclear strategists of the super-powers tend to set very high levels for 'credibility'. To match the enormous destructive power of the United States or the Soviet Union and possess a completely credible deterrent another power would, in their view, have to meet the following conditions. Its nuclear force would have to be large enough to inflict unacceptable damage on another nuclear power. It would have to possess a reliable means of delivery and be capable of penetrating any defence. It would have to develop its own damage-limiting capability, that is the capability to reduce or limit the damage expected from an enemy nuclear attack. This would mean an ability to attack enemy forces, intercept enemy aircraft or even missiles, or provide large-scale civil defence for the population.

It seems clear that China, with a defence expenditure roughly the same size as that of France, but with much larger conventional forces to maintain, cannot hope to reach such a level of development in the foreseeable future. She clearly could not expect for many years to be able to conduct a war on the scale possible to the United States which has the power 'not only to destroy completely her entire nuclear offensive forces, but to devastate her society as well'.[15]

It is possible to argue, however, for a different view of the credibility of national nuclear forces. A comparatively small

[15] Robert S. McNamara, Press Statement (USIS Text), 18 September 1967.

nuclear force, which was not designed to protect a large number of allies or meet a variety of contingencies, would by no means be the equal of the super-power forces in an actual conflict; it might still be thought to have a high deterrent value, out of proportion to its size, in confronting just such powers. The logic, or the psychology, of this is not appreciated by most American or Soviet strategists who continue to doubt the credibility of limited national nuclear forces. The super-powers also believe that the proliferation of nuclear weapons and the creation of national nuclear forces is obviously dangerous and destabilizing.

The Chinese have not publicly developed their views on nuclear deterrence but they certainly feel that the risks of war are not related to nuclear proliferation as such, but depend upon who obtains the weapons: in the hands of imperialist countries they are detrimental to peace; in the hands of socialist countries they are an aid to it.

An article in the *People's Daily* (5 April, 1968), for example, attacked the 'US–Japanese agreement for co-operation in nuclear energy'.[16] It argued that the Sato government was planning to equip the Japanese self-defence forces with nuclear weapons.

'As exposed by some Japanese socialist Diet members, the Sato government is studying the production of missiles with nuclear warheads under Japan's third arms expansion plan. In order to develop nuclear weapons in the service of US imperialism Sato and his gang have put up a smokescreen about the need to "deal with" China's "nuclear threat".'

After repeating that China would never be the first to use nuclear weapons, and adding a reminder that it was the United States which had first used atomic weapons on Japan, the article concluded with a general warning: 'We would like to warn the Japanese reactionaries: By following US imperialism and engaging in nuclear arming, and treading the old path of Hideki Tojo and company, you will be severely punished by the people of Asia and of the world, and will hasten your own doom.'

Such moralistic utterances, however, give very little insight into what an actual Chinese nuclear strategy is likely to be. It is possible to theorize that with a nuclear force which she thought credible China could expect to be able to deter an attack by

[16] 'No Nuclear Arming by Japanese Militarism Is Permissible', text in *Peking Review*, No. 16, 19 April 1968.

either the United States or the Soviet Union. It seems reasonable to assume that she would not try to achieve nuclear parity with either of the super-powers (any more than France or Britain intends to) but would seek to develop a force sufficiently powerful and with a delivery system adequate to threaten a number of American (or Soviet) cities. With such a force, which needless to say could also be used to threaten allies of the super-powers, she could perhaps hope to be able to deter an attack by either. That is to say, although China could not hope to match the total destructive capacity of the super-powers, she could hope to make the price of a nuclear attack on her so high as to make it unlikely that it would occur.

Such speculations, along with many detailed scenarios of nuclear conflicts involving China, cannot help having an air of unreality at present. China does not appear to be considering programmes to produce either long-range bombers or submarines as nuclear delivery vehicles, and in the absence of missile tests it is difficult to tell what nuclear strategy she is likely to pursue. If she were to concentrate on medium-range and intermediate-range missiles it would be suspected by her neighbours that they might be the targets. Both Japan and India might then feel compelled to develop their own nuclear programmes. If she were to develop an inter-continental ballistic missile capability the costs would be much greater and the American response probably more severe. An effective American anti-ballistic-missile (ABM) system would reduce the chances of a first-strike by China producing 'unacceptable damage'. The need to harden her own missiles, protecting them from blast effects of nuclear weapons by placing them in underground silos, and the whole problem of a second-strike capability would have to be considered.

The lack of public attention to such subjects in China is not in itself evidence that they have not been considered by China's military planners, but it is a reasonable assumption that the Maoist leadership would find most Western strategic thought alien in style and unpalatable in its conclusions. If they are to become full members of the World Nuclear Club they must nevertheless learn something of its language and theory if only to refute it. Michael Yahuda has plausibly argued that the necessity to consider the complexities of deterrence could force China out of her present isolation, that the interaction with the adversary which is inherent in strategic deterrence necessitates some communication about intentions, capabilities and strategies.[17] There is no evidence that this process has yet begun but it could begin shortly. It will be ironic if China's nuclear weapon, the supreme symbol of self-reliance, becomes the agent which destroys her self-sufficiency.

[17] Michael Yahuda, 'China's Nuclear Option', *Bulletin of the Atomic Scientists*, February 1968.

Chapter Five

BEYOND MAO

The Great Proletarian Cultural Revolution which dominated Chinese politics from the middle of 1966 until late in 1968 and which has not yet been formally terminated has had very uncertain effects inside the country. Abroad it has had one clear consequence : it has shaken or destroyed a number of assumptions about Chinese politics which have been very widely held outside China. The picture which had usually been taken for granted by the foreign student of China, and which in many ways was supported by the words of the régime itself, was something like the following. China was a nation reunified after forty years of turmoil by a Communist Party of enormous size which had totally penetrated its society. The leadership of the Party had been united by many years of revolutionary struggle and had been uniquely successful in avoiding the internal fratricide which had disfigured every other major Communist Party. The Party had won the allegiance of the Chinese masses and in many ways fundamentally transformed Chinese society, setting it on the way to complete modernization. This had required the imposition of totalitarian controls but these had been applied with psychological skill and a minimum of force.

There have always been students who have had reservations about one part or another of this presentation, but even the most conservative critics of the régime have usually conceded that the leadership has been remarkable by Communist or any other standards for its solidarity, persistence and sheer continuity. The main leaders had nearly all joined the Party very early in its history as students or comparatively young men. Despite some faction fighting in the 1920s and 1930s, once Mao Tse-tung had emerged as leader in 1935 a remarkable consensus had been achieved and only one minor purge had interrupted the smooth continuity of the leading group in power. This image has now been shattered for good. The air has been thick with fantastic charges, many of them self-contradictory and obviously untrue, aimed at key figures in the leadership. However much these charges may be discounted in themselves, the evidence of clique fighting, raging personal jealousy and destructive political infighting has been revealed to all the world. With political turmoil at the centre, strong fissiparous tendencies have appeared in the provinces; important local figures have struggled hard to preserve their regional power bases. Party cadres have been widely denounced as suffering from traditional bureaucratic vices and as having lost contact with the masses. The threat of political struggle turning to actual violence has hung heavily over the country. The army has become more and more involved in the problems of government. There have been many curiosities in this process which cannot be pursued here. What emerges most significantly is that the assumptions of those who, for good or ill, had accepted a model of Chinese society which showed it as a successfully working totalitarian system, have been severely challenged. The views of those who had always been sceptical about this model have been correspondingly strengthened. After all it would have been surprising if, after a century of dynastic decline, followed by almost forty years of warlordism, civil and foreign wars, during which no régime operated as an effective government for all of China, one political organization could have totally transformed this chaos and produced in a few years something so utterly unlike the traditional Chinese state. Perhaps the transformation has been more apparent than real? Perhaps the conservatives who said that you could not make a Communist state out of China were not completely mistaken?

There has certainly been a very common tendency to exaggerate the success of Communist educational and propaganda techniques in changing the fundamental cultural patterns of the country. It has surely been naïve to assume that because the whole country *appears* to have adopted a new set of beliefs that *in fact* they must be widespread; that because a highly centralized system of control over all communications media has made a new language almost universal that it expresses new universal convictions; that people so long accustomed to the difference between ritual performance and social reality have in fact all changed their basis patterns of thought and action. To put this in another way, it seems naïve to believe that the total politicization of the Chinese people, the peasantry in particular, has succeeded to anything like the extent which has been commonly predicated. Both the friends and enemies of the régime have tended to share a common delusion.

Without elaborating these points further it seems likely that any Chinese government is going to be concerned for a long time to come with problems about the stability and security of China which have no obvious connection with the rhetoric of Maoism. China is a vast political entity forced unwillingly in the last century to take part in a world of modern nation-states with which she had no fundamental sympathy. To use a slightly old-fashioned vocabulary, she is a country still struggling to find modern political institutions which can be made to work to preserve her traditional integrity.

The present Maoist leadership is full of contradictions. Mao undoubtedly provides charismatic leadership and a certain imperial style but he has a strong romantic and anarchic streak in his make-up which leads him to distrust all permanent organization and highly professional structures. He would seem to prefer an army of political enthusiasts, poorly equipped, to a body of cool professionals equipped with the most modern weapons. He would seem to prefer legions of politically educated students to multiple hierarchies of experts.

It is doubtful whether any modern state can be run on purely Maoist principles, let alone a state as large and complex as China. Mao himself has not got unlimited years to see if it can be done, and it is highly unlikely that he will be able to produce the revolutionary heirs he so earnestly desires to succeed him. It is clear that Mao himself is much concerned with this problem. His style of permanent revolution requires a constant new supply of revolutionary heirs. In principle these can always be found among the young but here the generation problem arises in a particularly acute form. Mao's own generation have been lifelong revolutionaries. They joined the Communist Party as students when they and it were both very young; they have aged with it. In common with the functionaries of Communist parties elsewhere they have been reluctant to face the dilemmas of a succession problem which in principle does not exist but in practice naturally does. In principle the Party chooses its leaders and will simply replace those who die by a process of election. In practice the self-selected leaders have always controlled the election process and no real institutional machinery exists for the selection of a new set of leaders. It is all very well for Mao to hope that the young will succeed him and his ageing colleagues but the people who will naturally see themselves as the next leaders are much more likely to be middle-aged cadres. About these middle-level and middle-aged cadres not a great deal is known. The old leadership has shown a very marked reluctance to add new blood to its immediate ranks. Even during the turmoil of the Cultural Revolution very few new faces have appeared near the top although many have disappeared.

According to the new draft constitution of the Party circulated in October 1968 'Comrade Lin Piao is Comrade Mao Tse-tung's close comrade-in-arms and successor'. Whether Comrade Lin will in fact be able to secure the succession remains to be seen, and even if he does succeed Mao in some formal sense, it is by no means certain that he will be able to continue Maoist internal policies of uninterrupted revolution and the constant creation of 'class' struggle. Bureaucratic pressures are likely to build up quickly against any leader without Mao's peculiar charisma. The need for orderly bureaucratic functioning and predictable administrative operations is likely to be much more strongly felt than the need for constant upheaval. This need not, however, involve any great repudiation of the Chairman's teaching. On the contrary one quite likely outcome would be for his name and writings to become completely sanctified. Just as the Kuomintang sanctified the name of Sun Yat-Sen and created a school ritual out of his last will and testament but then pursued policies which bore little relation to his own, so it is quite likely that the Communist Party of China will sanctify Mao's name and writings but adopt a much more bureaucratic style after his death.

What China so obviously needs is a less arbitrary style of politics. In this regard, Mao who sees himself as a great revolutionary has in fact had a profoundly reactionary influence. His oracular directives have often been as difficult to interpret as any classical text.[1] Where instructions are open to a large number of interpreta-

[1] Consider the following example of the later Maoist imperial style: 'The army should give military and political training in the universities, middle schools and the higher classes of primary schools, stage by stage

tions everything depends on the interpretation of key functionaries at any level.

The great Maoist truths are consistent with a very wide range of social facts and their application in particular instances has to be decided by someone. The Party generalist is here at an advantage over the technical expert; his rulings on political correctness can in fact be his technique for preserving his own power. The system in fact encourages a built-in arbitrariness which is inimical to rational administration. Those who have the power to decide what is politically correct also decide who is correct and who is not, and therefore who may proceed to do what. This use of arbitrariness as a political method to maintain personal control constitutes the essence of despotism. Whether it is justified by appeal to Confucian or Maoist truths its effect is the same.

The confusions of the Cultural Revolution illustrated such politics as their worst. The adulation of the Thought of Mao developed to the most extravagant lengths as everyone tried to prove their orthodoxy. Clearly some of the old-guard leaders had been harbouring anti-Maoist thoughts or at least sentiments but nobody wanted to be labelled an anti-Maoist. Maoism was orthodoxy and no one wanted to be heterodox. As new groupings multiplied they all denounced their opponents as anti-Maoist. Those who were attacked as anti-Maoist were naturally horrified and in turn denounced their attackers as the real anti-Maoists. These performances naturally puzzled outside commentators who

---

and group by group. It should help in re-opening school classes, strengthening organization, setting up the leading bodies on the principle of the "three-in-one" combination and carrying out the task of "struggle-criticism-transformation". It should first make experiments at selected points and acquire experience and then popularize it step by step. And the students should be persuaded to implement the teaching of Marx that only by emancipating all mankind can the proletariat achieve its own final emancipation, and in military and political training they should not exclude those teachers and cadres who have made mistakes. Apart from the aged and sick, these people should be allowed to take part as to facilitate their remoulding. Provided all this is done conscientiously, it is not difficult to solve the problems.'

'Directive Concerning the Great Strategic Plan for the Great Proletarian Cultural Revolution', 7 March 1967, republished March 1968. Text in *Peking Review*, No. 11, 15 March 1968.

tended to assume that the factions they perceived to be operating at any one time must have differing programmes. That they were in all likelihood politically unorganized groups with no real programme at all was very difficult to grasp.

The emergence of a political system in China in which real interest groups can gain expression may not seem a very likely development but if the country is to achieve economic modernization some modernization of politics is essential. The economic problems facing the country are enormous and no magic key to their solution is known to exist. The idea that the Communist Party of China has the secret of maintaining perfect industrial and agricultural discipline and effecting spectacular economic development has little left to justify it. Indeed the gloomier prognosticator might argue that the frustrations that the régime is likely to encounter in achieving a satisfactory rate of economic growth could well lead to an intensification of ideological politics rather than to any relaxation. A China frustrated in the achievement of reasonable national goals might well become even more doctrinaire in her proclamations of Chinese truth and virtue.

The idea of China as the doctrinal centre of the world with Maoist Thought as its epitome may serve some psychological purpose in China, however reactionary it may be, but Maoism is unlikely to be of much serious consequence in the rest of the world. No modern state can pretend to have a monopoly of truth and virtue. The early prophets of industrial society were wrong in assuming that the growth of science and industry would in itself lead to a decline of nationalism, and with the world in such an uneven state of development many states are likely to be moving into a stridently nationalistic phase as others are preparing to leave it.

The paradox of Maoism is that for all its self-proclaimed world significance it has been an extremely introverted and nationalistic doctrine. This does not make it irrational in the sense that its protagonists are totally insensitive to the consequences of their actions. Its oddities and stridency, however, have undoubtedly produced in many people a fear of an irrational, nuclear-armed China which in some cases assumes nightmare proportions. 'One source of this exaggeration' as Herman Kahn has suggested 'may be that many people are attempting consciously or unconsciously to find a new enemy to play the psychological and political role in internal and/or international politics that Stalin and the Soviet Union formerly did.'[2]

China, as this essay has stressed, is not likely to be a very plausible contender for such a role. She may, with luck, become the France of Asia but she is not in the foreseeable future going to become a super-power whether rational or not. The nightmare of a nuclear-armed China determined at any cost to assert herself in the world and obtain a great-power status consistent with her own view of her traditional importance has haunted numbers of Americans, Russians, Indians and Australians. No nightmare can be dispelled simply by argument but it is worth pointing out that in Japan, the Asian country with the most detailed knowledge of China, it is a nightmare very few people have. Japanese tend to express polite incredulity when this vision of China is unfolded to them. It is explicable, they tend to feel, only as one more example of the inability of non-Asians (even Indians) to understand Oriental political culture.

A nightmare of quite a different type is likely to haunt the historically-minded Chinese. In periods of great political and economic stress the old empire has more than once broken up into self-contained kingdoms. Regionalism has always been a powerful fissiparous force in Chinese politics and the great size and poor communications of the country provide natural bases for warlord régimes. Some critics were quick to hail the Cultural Revolution as the beginning of the end, seeing in the turmoil at the political centre all the traditional signs of the break-up of a dynasty. It was confidently asserted that the Party had been destroyed and nothing remained but pure military government. It is clear that this is far too simple an analysis but the possibility does exist that after Mao's death a violent succession struggle might occur in which attempts to settle old scores will lead to a *de facto* fragmentation of the country.

It seems much more likely, however, that a reorganized Party will struggle to preserve national unity at all costs and a programme of normalization will be widely agreed upon however much lip service is paid to the revolutionary canons of Maoism. The Communist Party of China will probably continue to proclaim in the words of the new draft Constitution that it 'firmly

[2] Herman Kahn and Anthony J. Wiener, *The Year 2000* (New York and London: Collier-Macmillan, 1967), p. 230.

adheres to proletarian internationalism, resolutely unites together with all the world's oppressed peoples and oppressed races of the whole world, each supporting the other, and each learning from the other, and struggles to overthrow imperialism headed by America, to overthrow modern revisionism headed by the Soviet revisionist renegade clique, to overthrow the reactionaries of all countries, to build a new world without imperialism, without capitalism and without any system of exploitation'. At the same time it could begin a less idealistic reassessment of its specific foreign-policy options.

While Mao is still alive it will be difficult to construct policies which conflict too flagrantly with his Grand Vision but it is not impossible to make many variations in policy seem consistent with it. One of the most influential figures in Peking is still Chou En-lai. Within his complex personality elements we tend to regard as disparate are held firmly together: he is always the 'correct' revolutionary; he is always loyal to Chairman Mao; he is also the embodiment of a great bureaucratic tradition and a natural diplomat. He still controls the apparatus of government and has many old friends and colleagues in the military and security establishments. He is the great survivor. With the eclipse of the old Party bureaucrats personified by Liu and Teng Hsiao-ping, and the apparent decline in influence of the vulgar radicals surrounding Chiang Ching (Madame Mao) the forces identified with Chou En-lai seem to be in the strongest position.

What could a government which was nominally Maoist but not in fact dominated by Maoist precepts expect to achieve in international affairs? It could without much difficulty improve diplomatic relations with many countries. The involvement of the diplomatic service in 'revolutionary activity' during the Cultural Revolution was probably as distasteful to many of the diplomats as it was to their hosts. It may have been necessary for many of them to prove their revolutionary virtue by showing their contempt for accepted canons of diplomatic behaviour but it did nothing to improve China's standing in the world. It could also turn its attention to the problems of formal representation and participation in international bodies. The position at the United Nations has been highly unrealistic for many years. China's seat is occupied by a régime whose chances of ever representing more than 1.5 per cent of the Chinese population are extremely slim, but while it has the support of the United States it cannot easily be removed from the United Nations any more than it can from Taiwan. The Communist government sees the United Nations as under the unholy domination of the United States and the Soviet Union. This attitude is not likely to change unless some break-through occurs on the question of Chinese representation. The probability of purely diplomatic activity effecting such a change is not great but as the years pass the claims of the United Nations to be a World Body while excluding Peking will become less and less defensible. The activities of the Soviet Union in cultivating in-formal relations with the Nationalists will, however, hardly im-prove the chances of a negotiated settlement.

It is unlikely that any type of 'two Chinas' solution, however much it appeals to outsiders, will be finally acceptable to any Chinese régime; any solution must at least give the appearance of unity restored and preclude any foreign interference. A successor to Chiang Kai-shek, even his son, might find it compara-tively easy to negotiate with the mainland once the idea of re-conquering it by military force has been given up. This pro-cess could be accelerated if China were to acquire the cap-ability to deliver nuclear weapons on the United States. As Geoffrey Jukes has suggested a Taiwan régime might then come to 'regard American support for Taiwan as somewhat less than certain, and seek an accommodation with the mainland government'.[3]

Taiwan could conceivably be given some sort of autonomous status as long as it was not the seat of a régime claiming to be the legitimate government of the whole country. Whether it could also be given representation in the United Nations on a basis com-parable to that of the Ukraine or Byelorussia would be un-important.

The fact that the United States does not formally recognize the régime in Peking has not meant that diplomatic contacts between them have been non-existent. On the contrary since the Panmunjon and Geneva Conferences the United States and China have conducted a long series of ambassadorial talks be-ginning in Geneva in 1955, and then transferring to Warsaw in 1958. This series has not been formally terminated and might

[3] Geoffrey Jukes, *The Strategic Situation in the 1980s* (Canberra: A.N.U. Press, 1968), p. 16.

well be resumed in 1969. The official record of the talks has, by agreement, remained secret but it has been possible for Ambassador Young to publish an impressive survey and discussion of them.[4] To the outside world they may appear to have been almost fruitless but they have had concrete effects in agreements between the two countries on the repatriation of civilians. It is true that the discussions on disarmament have been without result but at least some exchanges took place. Most important, although a just assessment is difficult without the full record, they have served to ease tension over Taiwan more than once and, in Young's words they have 'signalled intentions, established limits and prevented serious miscalculations' over Laos and Vietnam.[5] The continuation of such contacts could, at the very least, reduce the risks of future miscalculations between the two adversaries.

The resumption of talks would not in itself be likely to produce any great improvement in relations but it could help redefine the nature of the adversary relationship. It would be very difficult for the United States to make the adjustments to her position in the Far East which Peking would find desirable but there is nothing immutable about it. The extended American position in Asia resulted from World War II and its aftermath. It has been expensive to maintain and future administrations might well consider the cost not worth the benefits. If a reduction of American commitments seems at all likely China is unlikely to respond by adopting adventurist policies which might reverse it, that is which might provoke the United States, however unwillingly, into a major action against her. Even if a reduction of American influence in Asia could, in time, be achieved there is no way of achieving the removal of the Soviet Union. A future Chinese government might try to restore some meaning to the Sino–Soviet alliance but, while the memory of the events in Czechoslovakia in 1968 is still green, the prospects do not seem very bright. The Russian invasion of Czechoslovakia confirmed all its worst fears about the nature of Soviet leadership. The 'Socialist Imperialists', as they had been saying for a long time, were indistinguishable from the American imperialists and they may well have decided that the Soviet

[4] Kenneth T. Young, *Negotiating with the Chinese Communists: The United States Experience 1953–1967* (New York: McGraw-Hill, 1968).

[5] Young, *op. cit.*, p. 20.

Union presents a greater danger to them than the United States does. If this is the case it could be argued that in the long run it will be easier for China to improve her relations with the United States than with the Soviet Union. A Sino–American *détente* may be a long way off but the fact that it would increase Soviet uneasiness is not likely to make it less attractive in Chinese eyes. Despite its doctrinal rigidity Peking does not have a fixed assessment of the American threat. American policy statements are studied very carefully and apparent changes in American strategy are quickly noted. This fact is often obscured by the official style with which the government announces its comments on the American scene but what they do not say can be more significant than what they do. A settlement in Vietnam for instance which left any shred of American influence in the country would have to be opposed in public; but a settlement which appeared to give the United States a face-saving formula for withdrawal over a period of time, yet in fact provided the conditions for the final erosion of the American position there, would probably be covertly welcomed.

In the long run Vietnam is of no great importance to China compared with Japan, the real economic giant of the area. How to normalize relations with Japan and at the same time detach the Japanese from their dependence on the United States is a problem which will be with the Chinese for a long time. They are probably counting on the Japanese becoming increasingly interested in the advanced sector of the Chinese economy and, while protesting continuing friendship with the West, moving economically closer to China and militarily more distant from the United States. Here they may be disappointed. A highly developed Japan might well desire to cement her relationships with other highly developed countries rather than those like China whose economic prospects are doubtful.

Unsettled border issues may continue to provoke irritation or even minor wars like that with India in 1962, but none seems so highly charged as to provide occasion for a major war. Some Chinese may continue to harbour irredentist designs on Mongolia, but Mongolia's close dependence on the Soviet Union will probably deter any Chinese action. *163393*

The Sino–Soviet border has been a source of friction where Sinkiang abuts upon the Soviet Union, but its Far Eastern section presents a reasonable historical compromise, much of it naturally defined by waterways. It was in the eastern section, nevertheless, that the most recent fighting broke out in March 1969. At this time of the year the Ussuri River is frozen, thus making it easy for frontier guards of both sides to make contact with each other. The dispute has features typical of border incidents between countries whose relations are bad. Both sides claim intrusion by the other. Both claim provocation by the other. The territory in dispute is of little importance being, in this case, an island situated at a bend in the river. China has not renounced the river border although she describes the Treaty of Peking which established it in 1860 as 'unequal'. The Chinese case rests on an appeal to 'established principles of international law', according to which 'in the case of navigable boundary rivers, the central line of the main channel should form the boundary line which determines the ownership of islands. Chenpao Island and the near-by Kapotzu and Chilichin Islands are all situated on the Chinese side of the central line of the main channel of the Ussuri River and have always been under China's jurisdiction.'[6] A dispute about where the main channel of a river runs does not usually present any problem to two governments which want to settle it. If they do not want to settle it, it can of course be interminable.

Far to the south the remaining colonial enclaves of Hong Kong and Macao present a territorial problem of a different kind. As I have suggested their absorption will probably be deferred until the Chinese economy is a great deal stronger. For the immediate future the economic advantages of leaving them intact are considerable. When the lease of the New Territories which form the greater part of the Crown Colony of Hong Kong runs out in 1999 China may use the occasion to negotiate the absorption of the colony; but it is by no means certain she will want to do so even then.

For a long time to come the Chinese are likely to continue to see themselves as embattled, surrounded by enemies – on the one hand the treacherous Soviet Social Imperialists on the other the immensely powerful American Imperialists. No leading group in China is likely to advocate the sort of policies which would provoke a major attack by one or the other. Political tactics which

[6] See the notes accompanying the map frequently printed by China in March. Published, for example, in *Peking Review*, No. 12, 21 March 1969.

helped play one off against the other could conceivably have a traditional appeal to some, but the more doctrinaire are likely to continue to pin hopes on revolutionary theory. The capacity for limited and guerrilla-type wars to erode the strength of the enemy is keenly appreciated by the Chinese but nothing in Maoist doctrine, or in the thinking of the military professionals, makes it likely that Chinese policy will be directed to involvement in such affrays. Some will undoubtedly continue to advocate helping along the inevitable destruction of the capitalist system by giving limited arms and training assistance to foreign dissident groups, but this policy has not had the unanimous support of the leadership in the past and could again be opposed by the more cautious or the more economically minded. Any régime calling itself Communist will probably continue to pay lip service to the doctrine of continuous revolution in the Third World but this is very different from advocating or becoming involved in military adventures far afield.

Mao has sometimes talked as if China had a special role to play in the Third World between the socialist and imperialist camps, but her gestures of aid have been perfunctory and had little effect. The erosion of the two camps has not made this role seem more plausible. Mao, himself, has nevertheless been much concerned with his doctrinal pre-eminence. Attempts by the Soviet Government to undermine it and to encourage opposition to him among other Communist Parties and among Chinese Communists in and out of China, have hardly decreased his sense of doctrinal rectitude. At the height of the Cultural Revolution his followers professed to believe that all the Revolutionary Peoples of the world were hanging on his words.

Less doctrinaire successors might have what seems to outsiders a more realistic approach to international relations, but it does not follow that they will be easier to deal with; less doctrinaire successors could in fact be much tougher negotiators than the Maoists have been. It has been one of the arguments of this essay that Maoist policies have reflected an acute awareness of China's multiple weaknesses. A China after Mao which was economically and militarily stronger might still be no absolute match for the United States or the Soviet Union but she might feel strong enough to exert more direct power in Asia. Depending on the reactions of the great nuclear powers a nuclear-armed China might, as Alice Hsieh has argued, nevertheless find herself with fewer military options than before.[7]

The preceding analysis undoubtedly lacks the grand sweep of definitive theory. We are accustomed to seeing relations between nations in terms of power, and peace between nations maintained by different power systems, either by empire, by hegemony or by balance. We assume that China must fit into one of our categories and must see her security in terms of one of our systems. It is not at all clear that she does.

There is no real evidence that she sees herself in the crudest of these roles, the imperial, and that she plans to conquer alien people, subdue their governments and incorporate their territory. Tibetans, Uighurs and Mongols cannot be expected to share this view but there is no doubt that China saw her reimposition of control over their homelands as legitimate and a matter internal to China. On the other hand, it is quite unrealistic to see the millions of overseas Chinese as a potential extension of the Chinese *imperium*. The cultural links of these people with China have often been strong. They have formed minorities who have, naturally, looked on occasion to their homeland for a protection she has rarely been willing or able to extend. Their situation now varies greatly from one state in South-East Asia to another. They have been assimilated in large numbers in Thailand and small numbers in Australia. They have been actively persecuted in the Philippines and murdered in large numbers in Indonesia. They have had to adapt to many alien rulers, but in Singapore they have become sturdily independent. Their future clearly lies in adjusting where possible to the very different national conditions of the states in the area.

There is more plausibility in the view that China would like to establish a hegemonial position, that she sees herself as the natural leader of Asia, but there is little hard evidence for it. Her relations with her neighbours have been extremely variable and unpredictable. In recent years she has antagonized more than she has positively influenced.

China has viewed with great suspicion attempts by the Western powers to establish systems of equilibrium in Asia, regarding them

[7] See Alice L. Hsieh, Foreward to the Japanese Edition of *Communist China's Strategy in the Nuclear Era: Implications of the Chinese Nuclear Detonations* (Santa Monica: RAND Corporation), n.d., p. 22.

all as thinly disguised imperial exercises. She is most unlikely to consider joining any herself. The special variant of the balance of power which has been developed by the great nuclear powers – the balance of terror – is one which China may have to come to terms with, but she has not yet shown much inclination to do so. It would seem not unreasonable to conclude that, just as China has found it difficult to develop a modern political structure, so she has remained uncertain of her modern power role. In this situation she has maintained an essentially defensive military posture. It has been possible to reconcile this with Maoist military doctrine but the basic position has undoubtedly been obscured to some extent by an aggressively Maoist political stance.

DATE DUE

GAYLORD			PRINTED IN U S.A